Good ^C Lookin' Bachelors Cookbook

Published by Desperado Publishing
1133 South Riverside, Suite 10-122, Medford, OR 97501-7807
First printing 1996.
ISBN 0-9655419-0-8

5% of all profits from the sale of
Good Cookin' Bachelors Cookbook will go to the
Oregon Coalition Against Domestic and Sexual Violence.

Good Lookin' Bachelors Cookbook

Oregon Bachelors

Share Their Thoughts on Life, Love and Cooking

By

Lori Evans and Barb Velasquez

Edited by Les Melton
Designed by Cheryl L. Perry
Cover Photographs by John Revisky

DESPERADO PUBLISHING

1133 South Riverside, Suite 10-122
Medford, OR 97501-7807
(541) 773-7160

Since meeting three years ago, we have felt that we were destined to work on a project together. Our creative energies were so similar but we didn't know where to apply them. It wasn't until we began to see how difficult it is for women and men to meet that we realized our connection.

One winter day we were sitting around the kitchen table planning a Murder Mystery party that required four female and four male characters. We quickly formulated a list of potential female characters. Our problem surfaced when we realized we didn't know enough men to complete our invitation list.

After days of exploring our options, our list was finally complete. We recruited one family member, his married friend, a very flattered local convenience store clerk, coerced during a late night run for junk food, and a female friend who agreed to pose as a man.

The result of the party . . . everyone had a great time and the seed was planted for *Good Cookin' Bachelors*.

We hope our efforts will benefit others looking for that special someone!

                    – *Lori Evans and Barb Velasquez*

                      October 5, 1996

This cookbook is dedicated to all the single women and men
searching for that elusive soul mate and,
to the Oregon Coalition Against Domestic and Sexual Violence,
for keeping us focused on our journey.

A Special Thank You . . .

To our friends and family for your support . . . Rick, thank you
for getting the ball rolling . . . Rob, for your encouragement to
pick up the ball and run with it . . . Amy, now you can put your
seat belt on . . . Cheryl and John, your positive energy, creative
input and belief in us, has pushed us to new heights . . . SOWAC,
for making us define our mission over and over, and for
supporting women entrepreneurs . . . And, to the Good Cookin'
Bachelors participating in this book, for sharing yourselves.

TABLE OF CONTENTS

Preface

Acknowledgments

How to write to a bachelor

SECTION ONE
Breakfast Bachelors... 5

SECTION TWO
Lunch Bachelors.. 43

SECTION THREE
Dinner Bachelors 103

Index 181

Ordering information 185

HOW TO WRITE TO A BACHELOR

1. Select a bachelor from the cookbook.

2. Write a letter to the bachelor.

3. Place the letter in a stamped envelope with your return address and seal it. Your confidential letter will *not* be opened by *Good Cookin' Bachelors* or Desperado Publishing.

4. Address the envelope with the name of the bachelor and the page number where his photograph appears. See Example A.

Example A

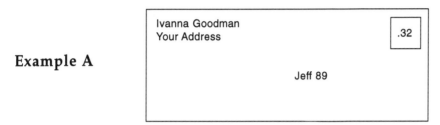

5. Place the addressed envelope from Example A into a second stamped envelope with your return address and send to *Good Cookin' Bachelors*. See Example B.

Example B

6. Upon receiving your letter to the bachelor, *Good Cookin' Bachelors* will attach the bachelor's address label to your letter and forward it to him.

SECTION ONE

Breakfast
Bachelors

JEFF

}
- Forty Something
- Public Safety and Emergency Medical Services
- Portland, Oregon

Hobbies and Interests . . .

"My hobbies and interests include athletic sports, such as team and tournament leagues, competitive shooting, mountain biking, running the Sawdust Trail at Glendoveer; and 'fixing things', like doing my own sewing and repairs... anything in the home, especially for my mom when she 'hints' about certain things."

Goals . . .

"To be the best person I can for myself and others. To always help those in need and offer resources and referral agencies to them as needed. To be a nurturing parent and spouse. This includes being the best father, 'papa' or 'daddy' for my children and always feel and comfort their needs."

– continued next page

5

Accomplishments . . .

"Being a father of two loving children in Idaho. Instructing seminars on public safety, personal safety, crime prevention, including 'safe dating'; abusive personalities; domestic violence prevention."

Philosophy of Life . . .

"My philosophy of life is be prepared. I'm neither a boy scout nor a survivalist, yet I believe in being able to respond and react to any situation that may arise in order to help others. I believe in the three R's: renurturing, rejuvenating, and restoring to maintain a 'reality check' on life."

Ideal Woman . . .

"My ideal woman has a healthy body-mind-spirit. She is loving, nurturing, romantic, sensuous, passionate with spontaneity. She loves to cuddle and is able to discern and reason logically; yet, will feel with her heart in decision making. She is supportive in maintaining discipline and accountability of family through love."

Jeff's Lowfat Weekend Booster Omelet
"Almost" Fat Free French Fries

JEFF'S LOWFAT WEEKEND BOOSTER OMELET ——————

– Serves 2

6 large eggs

6 slices Sizzlelean, beef or poultry

1 to 2 tablespoons canola oil

2 ounces part skim mozzarella cheese, grated

optional: diced tomatoes, mushrooms and green

peppers

1. In a frying pan on medium heat, cook Sizzlelean strips according to package instructions and place on a paper towel.
2. Separate eggs reserving 6 egg whites and 2 egg yolks (discard remaining 4 yolks). In a bowl, whip the 6 egg whites and 2 egg yolks.
3. Heat oil in a skillet on medium-high heat. Place Sizzelean strips in pan. Pour eggs over top.
4. Add optional items as eggs begin to solidify. Turn stove off.
5. Add cheese, fold and serve with fresh squeezed orange juice.

7

"ALMOST" FAT FREE FRENCH FRIES ———————————
– Serves 2

3 medium baking potatoes, peeled
non-stick canola oil cooking spray
1 large egg white
1 teaspoon of a favorite cajun spice

1. Slice each potato lengthwise into 1/4" oval, then slice ovals lengthwise into french fry strips.
2. Spray a baking sheet with non-stick cooking spray.
3. Mix egg white and spice in a bowl. Combine with potato strips, coating them well.
4. Spread potatoes evenly on cooking sheet and bake on bottom shelf of oven, 40-45 minutes at 400°.
5. Turn potatoes every 7 minutes with a spatula to brown evenly. Serve hot.

LENNY

- Fifty Something
- Businessman, Owner of Pyramid Juice Company
- Ashland, Oregon

Hobbies and Interests . . .

"My hobbies and interests include bicycling, cross-country skiing, dancing, hiking, theater, movies, traveling, fund raising and promoting youth oriented activities, being with my children, and expanding my self awareness."

Goals . . .

"My goals in life are to continue to enjoy life and to always feel good about my accomplishments and direction. I hope to continue to expand my business, be proud of my children's accomplishments, travel worldwide, and maintain my health in excellent form. My goal is also to meet a woman to share my life in joy and harmony."

– continued next page

Accomplishments . . .

"The accomplishments I'm proudest of are a Masters Degree in Engineering, working on the Lunar Module Project, designing the installation for the manufacture of the first IBM printed circuit memory boards, starting the Pyramid Juice company in the kitchen of my house and selling the juice nationwide, and fathering three beautiful children."

Philosophy of Life . . .

"My philosophy of life is to be honest, fair, and respect everyone for who and what they strive to be."

Ideal Woman . . .

"The qualities my ideal woman would have are to be physically attractive, intelligent, desire for spiritual and self awareness, non-smoker, financially and emotionally secure, physically active, enjoys outdoor and indoor sports, loves children, loves herself, and loves me."

Lenny's Breakfast Menu

Cottage Cheese Pancakes
Fruit Salad

COTTAGE CHEESE PANCAKES

– Makes 9 pancakes

"A creamy blintz, rich, without having to put in filling."

> 3 eggs
> 3 tablespoons flour (whole wheat or unbleached white)
> 1 pinch salt
> 1 cup cottage cheese

1. Separate eggs, beat egg whites until stiff; set aside.
2. Beat yolks with flour, salt, and cottage cheese.
3. Fold both mixtures together.
4. Grill or fry in greased frying pan.
5. Serve with pure maple syrup or your favorite jam. Garnish with oranges slices.

"Start the meal with a tall glass of 'Vegetable Cocktail,' Carrot or 'Green Juice.'
Have a cup of 'Oregon Berry Blast' or decaf coffee after the meal."

FRUIT SALAD

– Serves 4

"I chose it because it tastes good, has an attractive display, and is very healthy."

> 2 bananas
> 1 apple
> 1/2 pineapple
> 3 kiwis
> 2/3 cup fresh strawberries or blueberries in season
> 1/2 cup cashews
> 1 cup granola
> 8 ounces non-fat yogurt
> 2 tablespoons honey
> juice from 1/2 lemon

1. Cut all fruits into bite size pieces. Mix well in a large bowl.
2. Sprinkle cashews and granola on fruit.
3. For the salad dressing, mix yogurt, lemon juice, and honey together. Apply liberally to salad.

BEN

- Forty Something
- Wastewater Treatment
  Plant Operator
- Salem, Oregon

Hobbies and Interests . . .

"I have three young children, a daughter
16, a son 11 and another daughter 8, so a
lot of my interests revolve around them. I
spend a lot of time involved in their sports
programs, both as a coach and a spectator.
I enjoy salmon and steelhead fishing,
camping, and trips to the Oregon beach.
Nothing tastes better than a hot dog
cooked over a beach campfire. I also enjoy
flower gardening."

Goals . . .

"To raise my children to have good common sense and the ability to
think a situation through before making a decision. What a chore! Then,
look forward to retirement and maybe do some traveling to see, touch,
feel, and taste all the neat things that are out there in the world."

– *continued next page* 13

Accomplishments . . .

"Being the father of three great children. Last year coaching a 5th and 6th grade football team to an undefeated season and a city league championship. Being a former U. S. Marine and serving during the Vietnam War. Going back to college at age 34, for one year, and coming out fourth in my class."

Philosophy of Life . . .

"Always treat a person as you would want them to treat you. If something is on your mind, speak up about it and let your feelings be known."

Ideal Woman . . .

"My ideal woman has honesty, integrity, and a good sense of humor. I prefer a lady that likes to look nice and can go from Levi's to lace. She needs to enjoy children and quiet times alone. She is someone that doesn't use drugs and very little alcohol. She doesn't mind getting involved in things, is sports minded, and enjoys campfires at night."

Ben's Breakfast Menu

Smoked Salmon Omelette
Tropical Fruit Bowl

SMOKED SALMON OMELETTE ───────────────

– Serves 2

"I used to fish for salmon and steelhead trout quite a bit and was fairly successful at it, so I bought a smoker and learned to smoke fish. One morning, while at a friends house in California, on his wedding day, I was in charge of breakfast. Well, I had brought some of my smoked salmon with me and decided to try using it with eggs. It turned out great and everyone enjoyed it. Maybe you will too."

4 eggs
1/4 cup milk
3/4 cup grated cheddar cheese
1 cup crumbled smoked salmon
non-stick spray

1. Mix eggs and milk in a bowl.
2. Spray non-stick spray in a skillet. Pour in egg mixture and cook on medium-high heat until eggs are completely done.
3. Add the salmon and cheese, fold over, and cook for about 5 more minutes. Salt and pepper to taste.

TROPICAL FRUIT BOWL
– Serves 4

"Two years ago I made a trip to Hawaii on a working vacation. A co-worker and I were there to do some remodeling on his mother's condominium. This was one of the dishes she made for us that I enjoyed very much."

2 papayas, peeled and seeded
2 mangos, peeled and seeded
2 bananas
2 cups chopped fresh pineapple
1 lime
1 tablespoon honey
shredded coconut, as desired
shredded almonds or macadamia nuts

1. Cut all fruit into bite size pieces, place in a medium size bowl.
2. Take the juice of one lime, add honey, then blend.
3. Add honey and lime mixture to fruit, mix until well coated.
4. Sprinkle with coconut and nuts.

MARK

- Thirty Something
- Corporate Spray Technician/
  Area Coordinator
  Excel Communications
- Central Point, Oregon

Hobbies and Interests . . .

"I enjoy weight training and body building to keep me in shape for all of the other interests I have. I love winter sports such as snowboarding and, in the summer, surfing, water skiing, camping, and mountain biking. I am open to anything fun or relaxing."

Goals . . .

"To stay happy and healthy and maintain financial security. I own my own home but, I hope to someday design and build the home of my dreams. I want to find a woman who appreciates a real nice guy."

– continued next page

Accomplishments . . .

"My 11 year old son, Travis, who is the best thing that ever happened to me. I have two excellent careers and I am doing well in both!"

Philosophy of Life . . .

"Work hard, be honest, and have as much fun as you can because you don't get many second chances."

Ideal Woman . . .

"Honesty above all. Someone with a good sense of humor and a nice smile. Someone who is self sufficient and sure of themselves. She would be athletic in stature and enjoy being active, spontaneous, and a true romantic."

Mark's Breakfast Menu

Quick-N-Easy Breakfast Burritos
Flapjacks
French Toast

QUICK-N-EASY BREAKFAST BURRITOS

– Makes 4-5 burritos

1 15-ounce can roast beef hash

6 eggs

4 or 5 large flour tortillas

cheddar cheese, grated for 4 burritos

salsa, as desired

non-stick cooking spray

1. Heat hash in a frying pan over medium heat until it begins to brown, stirring frequently, then keep on lowest heat.
2. Spray a second pan with non-stick cooking spray then scramble eggs on medium heat.
3. Heat flour tortillas for half a minute in your microwave or on lowest temperature in a conventional oven for 5 minutes
4. Put desired amount of hash, egg, cheese and salsa. Roll it all up and enjoy.

19

FLAPJACKS

– Serves 2

"These are not like conventional pancakes because they are thinner and more crepe like...very addicting!"

> 2 eggs
> 1/2 teaspoon salt
> 1 cup milk
> 1/2 cup all-purpose flour
> non-stick cooking spray

1. Combine first three ingredients and mix thoroughly using a whisk.
2. Add flour slowly and continue to mix, creating a thin and runny batter. If it is too thick, add more milk.
3. Coat a skillet with non-stick cooking spray and heat on medium-high.
4. When the pan is hot, spoon enough of the batter to create a 6" or 7" flapjack. Use the bottom of your spoon to spread out the mixture.
5. When outer edges become lightly brown and curl upwards, flip it over using a spatula. It will cook very fast to a thickness of about 1/8".
6. As you finish cooking your flapjacks, keep them on a plate with a large bowl over the top.

Flapjacks can be enjoyed served with the following:

1. Top with butter and your favorite syrup.
2. Add blueberries, sliced strawberries, or peaches, or spoon your favorite fruit filling over them with some whipped cream.
3. My favorite way - eat them rolled up with (some favorite) homemade jam.

FRENCH TOAST

– Serves 2

"This is one of my favorite breakfast recipes handed down from my mom."

> 2 eggs
> 1/4 cup milk
> 1/2 teaspoon vanilla extract
> 1/4 teaspoon nutmeg
> cinnamon, as desired
> butter or margarine spread
> powdered sugar, as desired
> 4 slices of fresh French bread cut to 1" slices

1. In a shallow bowl, mix eggs, milk, vanilla, and nutmeg until thoroughly combined.
2. Spray a large skillet with non-stick cooking spray and place on medium heat. (NOTE: a large skillet will hold 4 slices of bread.)
3. Dip bread into mixture (be sure not to let bread soak in mixture), then quickly flip to other side, remove and place on heated skillet.
4. While one side of bread is cooking, sprinkle some cinnamon on the uncooked side. Allow a couple of minutes to cook then check that the cooked side has turned a golden brown. Flip it over with a spatula. The second side will cook faster because the pan is hotter.
5. After browning the second side, remove from pan and add butter, powdered sugar and your favorite syrup.

BOB

 · **Forty Something**
· **Engineering Specialist**
· **Medford, Oregon**

Hobbies and Interests . . .

"I play guitar and sing, with my favorite song being 'Windmills of Your Mind'. I go folk dancing on Fridays. I swim five times a week. I collect unusual news articles, cartoons, and distribute them to friends."

Goals . . .

"At 49, I feel I have met life and emerged successful. I lead a stable life, eat well (I'm a good cook), and feel modestly successful. I am well educated, enjoy many friends, and have found a home and area in which to celebrate life. If there is one goal left, it is to get involved in a permanent relationship, though at 49, it obviously doesn't dominate my life."

– continued next page

23

Accomplishments . . .

"The accomplishments I'm proudest of are that I can look back on my development years and quietly smile to myself...that I've reached this point and have developed a stable lifestyle...that I still have a positive outlook on life...that I'm enjoying this journey rather than being driven by endpoints."

Philosophy of Life . . .

"We are all bodies of energy, flaring out during joy and clinging close during storms. I try to increase the energy level in myself and others through humor, alertness, sensitivity, and love. I can increase my own energy level for a longer period by raising the level of those around me rather than concentrating on myself."

Ideal Woman . . .

"I would enjoy a woman who lives and works with quality in mind rather than quantity. Someone who has a musical soul, enjoys a healthy lifestyle, and good conversation."

Bob's Breakfast Menu

Omelette Deluxe
Papa's Porridge
Bob's Blender Mix

OMELETTE DELUXE

– Serves 1

2 eggs

2 large mushrooms, sliced

fresh garlic, as desired

1/8 medium onion, diced

1/2 cup grated sharp cheddar cheese

1/8 cup water

1 teaspoon oil

salsa, as desired

1. Mix eggs, mushrooms, garlic, onion, and cheese.

2. Heat frying pan on high until a drop of water instantly sizzles.

3. Add oil to water, mix and pour into frying pan. Quickly add the egg mix, cover and turn off the heat.

4. Let sit for 5 to 10 minutes. Mixture will continue to cook as it cools down.

5. Top with salsa.

PAPA'S PORRIDGE BREAKFAST

– Serves 2

"The main ingredient of this meal is a mixture called Papa's Porridge. I get it at a natural food store in Eugene, or you can make your own."

The combination of dry ingredients should equal 1 1/2 cups:

rolled oats, as desired

raisins, as desired

walnuts, as desired

oat bran, as desired

dried apple, as desired

cinnamon, to taste

2 cups milk

2 tablespoons molasses

4 mango slices

1. In 2 microwave safe bowls place 3/4 cup of Papa's Porridge mix. Add 1 cup of milk to each.
2. Cover each bowl with a saucer and place on a platter, as it overflows when cooking.
3. Heat in microwave on high for 2 minutes and let sit for 2 minutes.
4. Add 1 heaping tablespoon of molasses and 2 mango slices to each and stir, chopping up mango as you stir.

BOB'S BLENDER MIX

– Serves 2

"I have this every meal that I'm home and I never get tired of it."

1 banana
1 apple, cored
1 cup milk

1. Put banana, apple, and milk in a blender.
2. Blend for 10 seconds.

Variations: add ice to make a frozen fruit shake.

27

MIKE

- Forty Something
- USDA Forest Service Timber Cruiser
- Jacksonville, Oregon

Hobbies and Interests . . .

"My hobbies and interest include hiking, bicycling, reading, working with computers and computer games, studying and identifying plants and animals. I also enjoy drinking coffee in the morning, observing nature and visiting and working with people."

Goals . . .

"My goals in life are staying healthy, active, working and happy. My career goal is to work in the fields of ecology and biology. Personal goals include purchasing a country home, designing and remodeling homes and sharing my life experiences with that special someone."

– continued next page

Accomplishments . . .

"The accomplishments I'm proudest of are receiving a Bachelors of Science degree in Ecology and Systematic Biology from California Polytechnic State University, San Luis Obispo, California in 1995; receiving an Associates of Arts degree from Modesto Junior College, Modesto, California in 1991; completing a two year program in Architectural Drafting and Building Construction at Mitchell Vocational Technical School, Mitchell, South Dakota in 1981; working for four seasons as a Recreation Technician for the USDA Forest Service, Hathaway Pines, California; improving the native fish populations of the upper Midwest, while working for four seasons at Gavin's Point National Fish Hatchery, Yankton, South Dakota; working with my brothers building new houses in South Dakota and sharing a happy childhood with many brothers and sisters on the family farm/ranch in east central South Dakota."

Philosophy of Life . . .

"My philosophy of life is to be happy, honest and real, maintain a good sense of humor; to always look at the positive side of life and experience the joy of working with other people; to accept change and continue to work towards self improvement."

Ideal Woman . . .

"The qualities my ideal woman would have are to be honest, caring, loving, and in good health; to have high self esteem, enjoy laughter, outdoor activities and nature, walking, talking, children and people."

Southern Cornmeal Griddle Cakes with Strawberry Sauce
Good Eggs

SOUTHERN CORNMEAL GRIDDLE CAKES

– Serves 2

"This is a wonderful hotcakes meal served with a fruity strawberry sauce. I enjoy preparing and eating this meal on weekends, when I have additional time (smile), and on cold winter mornings."

1 1/2 cups unsifted all-purpose flour

3/4 cup yellow cornmeal

2 tablespoons sugar

4 1/2 teaspoons baking powder

1 teaspoon salt

2 cups milk

1 large egg or 1/4 cup egg substitute

1/4 cup vegetable oil or melted
   vegetable shortening

1. In a medium size bowl, stir together the flour, cornmeal, sugar, baking powder, and salt.

2. Heat a non-stick or lightly oiled griddle to medium heat or an electric skillet to 150°, or until a little water sprinkled on the surface skitters.

3. In a small bowl combine the milk, egg, and vegetable oil. Combine with dry ingredients until thoroughly mixed.

4. Pour batter 1/3 cup at a time onto hot griddle. Cook until bubbles form on the surface of the griddle cake. Turn and cook until the underside is brown.

5. Transfer to a serving dish and place in a warm oven until all the griddle cakes are cooked. Top with strawberry sauce and whipped cream, if desired.

31

STRAWBERRY SAUCE

– Yields 2 3/4 cups

2 10-ounce packages frozen, unsweetened strawberries

1/3 cup sugar

1/4 cup water

2 tablespoons cornstarch mixed with 1/4 cup water

1 teaspoon vanilla extract

1. Remove frozen strawberries from package and let stand at room temperature for 10 minutes.
2. Cut partially frozen strawberries into thick slices and place in a medium size saucepan. Add sugar and water. Cook over medium-low heat, stirring frequently, until thawed.
3. Increase heat to high, stirring constantly, bring to a boil. Gradually pour cornstarch mixture into strawberry mixture, stirring constantly. Cook several minutes continue stirring until mixture boils, thickens, and turns translucent.
4. Remove from heat and stir in vanilla.

GOOD EGGS

– Serves 4

"This is a delicious egg dish that can be served at any time. They are especially good after a relaxing morning walk. This meal is one of my favorites because it's easy to make and tasty. In addition, I have received many positive comments on the great taste of Good Eggs."

1/4 small white onion, sliced

1/2 cup mushrooms, sliced

1/2 stick butter

6 eggs

1/4 cup milk

1/8 teaspoon black pepper (optional)

1/4 cup cheese, cubed or thinly sliced

1 or 2 tomatoes

1. Brown onion and mushrooms in 1/8 stick of butter over medium heat; remove from pan and set aside.

2. Beat eggs and milk together, adding black pepper.

3. In a medium size non-stick skillet, melt remaining butter over medium heat. Add egg mixture to skillet and immediately reduce heat to low. Add mushrooms, onion, and cheese.

4. When top of egg is almost set but still moist, fold the eggs with a spatula. Flip to opposite side. Remove from heat as soon as eggs are fluffy. Serve with sliced tomato.

STEVE

- Forty Something
- CEO, The Kodel Group and
  Retired Air Force Officer
- Grants Pass, Oregon

Hobbies and Interests . . .

"I've slept under the stars at Crater Lake
and among the Redwoods near the coast. I
ran the 'River Wild'—mostly backward,
and hiked way too many trails. I love
watching high school football...I also
enjoy seeing a few Ducks' games. I
challenged the bunny trails at Mt.
Ashland, then bought myself some roller
blades...I greet each morning with a slow
jog then visit the gym for a fast burn. I love to relax in the evening
watching my favorite sitcoms. I love comedy clubs and especially enjoy
the romance of the theater..."

Goals . . .

"I set lots of goals. It's a great way to test myself and it certainly makes
my life richer. Too often, people stand on the sidelines. It's so much
better to be in the game! My goals are simple—to be successful in love,
life and business. In love, I'd like to be wanted not needed; in life, I'd like
to have made a difference, and, in business, I'd like not to meet myself
coming and going."

– *continued next page*

Accomplishments . . .

"Certainly and foremost in my mind is the completion of my distinguished Air Force career. Then, there is my gold medal showing in the shot put and javelin at Seoul's Olympic Park in 1992, and subsequent selection to the 1993 Air Force track team and Male Athlete of the Year honors. I am also proud of having finally completed graduate school, earning my MBA, and starting my companies: Lare Corporation, Polar Corporation, and Kodel Group. But, I am most proud of my three sons and how they are turning out."

Philosophy of Life . . .

"Always dream the dream. Don't wait for opportunity to knock—sneak in the window if you have to. You have two choices. You can get busy living or you can get busy dying. Always believe in yourself, no matter what! Take nothing for granted, especially those you love."

Ideal Woman . . .

"That's easy—Jamie Buchman!! My ideal woman has a wonderful sense of humor. Her smiles, tickles and grins give meaning to my life. She never throws things and only occasionally pouts. She's tender, pretty and bright, independent, yet vulnerable at night. She's not too sensible, confused, or messy. She's supportive of my dreams while chasing her own . . . My ideal woman is sexy and passionate and affectionate. She has a pure heart and giving nature with a delicious appetite for love and life . . . My ideal woman has a lightly freckled nose and sensuous look. She has a bouquet smile, compassionate touch, and eyes that dance with the moon. . . "

Steve's Breakfast Menu

**Peach Shortcake
Turkey and Apple Sausage
Hot Grape Nuts
Spicy Tomato Sipper**

PEACH SHORTCAKE

— Makes 10 servings

1 cup all-purpose flour	1/4 cup milk
1 teaspoon baking powder	1/4 teaspoon vanilla
1 tablespoon sugar	non-stick cooking spray
1/2 teaspoon cinnamon	3 medium peaches, peeled, pitted and sliced
1/4 cup margarine or butter	or 1 16-ounce can sliced peaches, drained
1 egg white, slightly beaten	1/2 cup vanilla non-fat yogurt

1. In a medium mixing bowl stir together flour, baking powder, sugar, and cinnamon.

2. Cut in margarine until mixture turns to course crumbs. Make a well in the center.

3. In a separate bowl combine egg white, milk, and vanilla; pour into the flour mixture. Stir until dough sticks together.

4. Coat a 9" pie plate with non-stick cooking spray. Press batter evenly into pie plate.

5. Bake at 350° for 20 to 25 minutes or lightly browned. Cool.

6. Chop 2 peach slices and stir into the yogurt. Arrange remaining peach slices over top of shortcake. Spoon yogurt mixture over the top of shortcake. Serve warm.

TURKEY AND APPLE SAUSAGE

– Serves 2

1/2 pound ground turkey

1/2 cup grated apple

2 tablespoons bread crumbs

1/4 teaspoon crushed sage

1/4 teaspoon ground pepper

1 pinch salt

1 pinch nutmeg

1 pinch paprika

non-stick cooking spray

1. In a large bowl, combine all ingredients. Make into four 1/2" thick patties.

2. Spray a large skillet with non-stick cooking spray. Cook the sausage patties over medium heat for 8 to 10 minutes or until inside is done.

HOT GRAPE NUTS

"It's a great, fat free, hot cereal your family will love."

1/4 skim milk
1/4 cup Grape Nuts
fresh fruit or honey, as desired

1. Place 1/4 cup Grape Nuts cereal in a microwavable bowl; add skim milk.
2. Microwave on high for 1 minute.
3. Add fresh fruit or honey.

SPICY TOMATO SIPPER
– *Serves 2*

"I choose this drink once in awhile, as you just have to live on the edge sometimes"

2 cups tomato juice

2 tablespoons lemon juice

1 teaspoon Worcestershire sauce

1/2 teaspoon horseradish

hot pepper sauce, to taste

ice cubes

2 celery sticks

1. In a pitcher stir together tomato juice, lemon juice, Worcestershire sauce, horseradish, and hot pepper sauce.
2. Pour mixture into glasses of ice. Garnish with celery sticks.

SECTION TWO

Lunch
Bachelors

DEREK

- Thirty Something
- Cook/Pro Musician
- Oregon City, Oregon

Hobbies and Interests . . .

"The first and only thing that I love is music! I love to write songs on my guitar and perform for people, making them feel good."

Goals . . .

"My goals in life are very simple. As corny as it sounds, I just want to be happy. To find someone who enjoys music as much as I do and continue making music..."

Accomplishments . . .

"One stands out and that was in August of 1992, when the Grateful Dead cancelled a show in Eugene. A band I was involved with got to play that show in front of 16,000 people. It was the greatest feeling ever. I am very proud to have done that!"

– continued next page

Philosophy of Life . . .

"Give one another a break, relax and take time to compromise with people. Try to be happy and make the best out of what you have. Remember, when you're down things can only look up. Make it better and it will be better. We control our own fate, life can be great."

Ideal Woman . . .

"My ideal woman is never the jealous type. She has pride in herself, dislikes fighting, and is willing to work on the relationship. She is loving and likes to cuddle. Someone who loves music and movies of all types and is creative in bed...would not mind having some lazy days lounging in bed. She knows how to relax, no stress, no drama. Could this be you?"

Spectacular Squash
Yoshida's Chicken

SPECTACULAR SQUASH

– Serves 6

1 8-ounce package herb seasoned cornbread stuffing mix

1 stick of butter, melted

2 pounds zucchini, sliced (6 cups)

1/2 large onion, sliced

1 10 1/2-ounce can cream of chicken soup, no water added

1 cup sour cream

1 cup grated carrots

1. Combine 1/2 of cornbread stuffing mix with butter and press into a 9" x 13" dish.
2. Lightly steam zucchini and onion, cooking only slightly, and set aside.
3. Mix soup and sour cream together, stir in carrots, zucchini, and onion.
4. Spread vegetable mix in dish and top with remaining cornbread stuffing.
5. Bake at 350° until bubbly or brown, approximately 30 minutes.

YOSHIDA'S CHICKEN ──────────────────────
– Serves 2

"I got this recipe from my mother...thank goodness for moms."

       8 skinless, boneless chicken thighs
       1 tablespoon vegetable oil
       1/4 cup Yoshida's Gourmet Sauce

1. In a large skillet, brown chicken in vegetable oil over medium-high heat.
2. Add sauce, simmer for 20 minutes.

PAUL

- Sixty Something
- Marriage and Family Therapist
- Ashland, Oregon

Hobbies and Interests . . .

"My hobbies and interests include a significant interest in keeping physically and emotionally fit. I do this enjoyably through moderate mountain biking and easy jogging on forest trails, along with mild workouts at the racquet club. I enjoy cooking, dancing, and reading, particularly books on relationships, communication, personal enhancement, and books on travel."

Goals . . .

"My goals in life are to live my life fully. Part of making this happen is my intention to be more present and fully experience myself, others I'm with, and where I'm at. I also intend to go to many places I've never been and do activities I've never done. It is my desire to assist others to empower themselves to fully live lives of their choosing. While doing

– continued next page

47

this I plan on becoming more like the Velveteen Rabbit, as I believe what the skin horse told him, 'Once you become real it lasts always'."

Accomplishments . . .

"Several accomplishments I'm pleased to have made are moving from Los Angeles to the San Francisco bay area in 1973, going back to college, obtaining a degree in Psychology, and becoming a Licensed Marriage, Family and Child Therapist. I now do some work with men who abuse children and believe I accomplish a lot by assisting them to eliminate this behavior— a change that benefits women and children as well as men."

Philosophy of Life . . .

"My philosophy and some of the guiding principles of my life are that I am responsible for just about everything that seemingly happens to me. I create happiness, dis-ease, conflicts, joys, bliss, and personal peace. It is my intention to benefit from adversity. I believe in experiencing my feelings— all of them, with most to be enjoyed and some to pay attention to and receive the message they give me. For me to be true to myself and authentic with others, I believe in sharing much of what I feel."

Ideal Woman . . .

"The qualities my ideal woman would have are that she would feel good about herself, could and does take care of her emotional self and physical body, and, yet, can be vulnerable and enjoy being taken care of. She likes natural activities. She is a lady who has the desire and the time to develop a caring relationship."

Paul's Lunch Menu

Carrot Apple Delight Soup
Pineapple Pumpkin Bread
Peanut Mousse Cheese Pie
Ben and Bailey's Smoothie

CARROT APPLE DELIGHT SOUP

"One of the most delightful tasty meals I have ever enjoyed. It can be an entire meal or soup course. If served as a soup course, the main meal better be exquisite or it will be a let down."

– Yields 1 quart

1 Forrest Gump soundtrack tape	1/4 cup plus 2 tablespoons apple juice
1 cup diced onion	2 tablespoons dry white wine
1 cup diced carrot	1/4 cup whipping cream
1 cup diced celery	1/3 cup flour
2 cloves garlic, minced	1/4 cup diced tomatoes
2 1/2 teaspoons curry powder	1 tablespoon lemon juice
2 tablespoons butter	1/2 heaping cup peeled and diced apple
2 2/3 cups chicken stock	1 dance partner

1. Start the tape.
2. Saute' onions, carrots, celery, garlic, and curry powder in 1 tablespoon butter until tender.
3. Add chicken stock, apple juice, white wine, and whipping cream. Bring to an easy boil. This is a good time to ask co-cook for a dance.
4. In a separate pan, melt remaining butter, add 2 to 3 tablespoons of liquid from cooking soup and slowly stir in flour. When it is no longer lumpy, pour flour mixture into soup. Simmer until slightly thickened.
5. Add tomatoes, lemon juice, and apples. Simmer only about 5 minutes so apples stay crisp.

49

PINEAPPLE PUMPKIN BREAD ————————————————

"I like this tasty treat as it is pretty healthy and keeps me from partaking of other less healthy snacks."

1 cup whole wheat flour

3/4 cup all-purpose flour

1 1/2 teaspoons baking soda

1/2 teaspoon cloves

1/2 teaspoon nutmeg

1 teaspoon cinnamon

1/2 teaspoon allspice

1 1/2 cups canned pumpkin

1/2 cup salad oil

2 eggs

1/2 cup honey

1/3 cup water

1/2 cup crushed pineapple

1/2 cup diced dates

1/2 cup diced walnuts

1. Mix dry ingredients together.
2. Add all other ingredients and mix.
3. Place in a greased loaf pan, fill about 60% full.
4. Bake at 325° from 50 to 90 minutes depending on pan size. The bread is done when a knife is inserted and comes out clean.

"Sometimes I spread about 1/4 inch of pineapple on a slice and then eat it."

PEANUT MOUSSE CHEESE PIE

– Makes 1 pie

"This pie is delightfully smooth...great for potlucks and you can have small pieces and be satisfied."

> 20 to 25 chocolate wafers
> 2 tablespoons whole unsalted peanuts
> 1/3 cup chopped unsalted peanuts
> 3 tablespoons melted butter
> 1 8-ounce package lite cream cheese, room temperature
> 1/2 cup chunky peanut butter
> 1/4 cup honey
> 1/3 cup sugar
> 3/4 cup whipping cream

1. Crush chocolate wafers and 2 tablespoons of peanuts into fine crumbs, making about 1 cup. Put into a 9" pie pan and stir in 1/3 cup chopped peanuts and butter. Firmly press mixture over bottom and sides of pan.
2. Bake at 350° for approximately 10 minutes. Let cool.
3. With an electric mixer, blend cream cheese, peanut butter, honey and sugar.
4. In another bowl, whip cream until fluffy, then lightly fold into pie mixture.
5. Spoon mixture into crust, cover and refrigerate overnight.

BEN AND BAILEY'S SMOOTHIE

– Serves 2

"I chose this drink as once in a while you have to break out and do it."

4 scoops Ben and Jerry's ice cream, any flavor(s)

3 tablespoons Bailey's Irish Cream

1 small banana

2 tablespoons hot fudge sauce

   (I use Mrs. Richardson's non-fat sauce.)

milk, as desired

1. Blend all ingredients in a blender, adding a little milk at a time until it is desired consistency.
2. Serve in liqueur glasses to add to the delicacy of the experience.

MARK

} • Thirty Something
• Fence Builder
• Gold Beach, Oregon

Hobbies and Interests . . .

"I grew up on the Oregon coast, and have always loved the outdoors. I enjoy hiking, backpacking, camping, canoeing, gardening, fruit growing, and harvesting wild foods. I also enjoy reading, writing letters, keeping a neat house and cooking. I like to keep myself in good physical condition."

Goals . . .

"I want to live my life in a way that's pleasing to God, being used by him to bless others as I do his will. I want to do what's right, no matter what everyone else is doing. I would like to find my 'niche' in this world and fulfill all the potential God has given me."

– continued next page

53

Accomplishments . . .

"I planted an orchard of 35 apple, pear, plum, and cherry trees in 1983, that now produces most of my family's fruit. In 1985, I built almost a mile of the Oregon Coast Trail by myself. In my hometown of Gold Beach, I'm known as one of Curry County's best fence builders."

Philosophy of Life . . .

"I believe in a simple lifestyle of hard work, honesty, and Christian values. Making a lot of money and being 'successful' in the worldly sense is not a priority in my life. This life is pretty short, really. I don't want to get so involved in the 'cares of this world', that I lose sight of the eternal picture."

Ideal Woman . . .

"To me the 'ideal woman' would be a very kind, caring, honest, intelligent, and loving person who likes herself and loves the Lord Jesus. She would be 23-33 years old, preferably tall, reasonably slim, and healthy. She'd have good moral values, along with a positive attitude and good sense of humor. She should be attractive (to me at least). Last, but not least, she must love the outdoors."

Mark's Lunch Menu

Mark's Hamburger Pizza
Apple Pie Bars

MARK'S HAMBURGER PIZZA

– Makes 1 large pizza

"Hearty beef pizza for big appetites! I like to make it, then heat up the leftovers for several days."

For the crust:
2 cups all-purpose flour
1 cup lukewarm water
1/2 teaspoon yeast

1. Dissolve yeast in lukewarm water. Add flour and mix until dough forms.

2. Knead on a floured surface.

3. Let dough sit for 1 hour, then roll it out and put in a greased, 10" x 15" pan.

For the topping:
1 pound hamburger
1 large onion, chopped
1 15-ounce tomato sauce
oregano, as desired
12 ounces mozzarella cheese, grated

4. Brown hamburger and onion in a frying pan.

5. Pour tomato sauce on the crust and sprinkle with oregano. Add the hamburger. If desired, add pepperoni, olives, mushrooms, etc.

6. Cover with mozzarella cheese and bake at 400° for 20 to 25 minutes. Cut into squares and eat!

55

APPLE PIE BARS

"Just like apple pie...only better! Luscious apple filling, surrounded by tender, flaky crust!"

For the crust:

2 1/2 cups flour

1 tablespoon sugar

1 teaspoon salt

1 cup margarine or butter

1 egg yolk plus milk to equal 2/3 cup of liquid

For the filling:

6 cups sliced apples

1/2 cup sugar

1 teaspoon cinnamon

1 tablespoon flour

For the frosting:

1 cup powdered sugar

1/4 cup margarine or butter

1 teaspoon vanilla

milk, as desired

1. Mix flour, sugar, and salt. Cut in margarine until it balls up.
2. Add egg yolks and milk; mix well.
3. Cut dough into 2 halves. Press one half into a 10" x 15" greased pan.
4. Combine filling ingredients together and put into crust.
5. Roll out top crust on wax paper then place over the top of the filling.
6. Cut slits in top crust and bake at 375° for about 45 minutes or until brown. Remove from oven and cool.
7. Combine powdered sugar, margarine, vanilla, and just enough milk to make it blended and smooth. Spread over the top crust.
8. Cut into squares and serve.

PAUL

- Thirty Something
- Direct Care
- Grants Pass, Oregon

Hobbies and Interests . . .

"My hobbies and interests include being outdoors, hunting, fishing (especially fishing), rock hunting, and traveling. I take two or three trips a year to Montana to camp, fish, and hunt. I enjoy drinking coffee with friends and I also read a lot."

Goals . . .

"My goals in life are to go fly fishing in Scotland, catch a 10 to 15 pound Rainbow on a fly rod, spend time with someone who's nice, make enough money to pay the bills and have a little left over for myself. I want to be happy and find a bottle of single malt scotch older than myself."

– continued next page

GOOD COOKIN' BACHELORS COOKBOOK

Accomplishments . . .

"The accomplishments I'm proudest of are having a good daughter, fly fishing in Montana, and making it this far without spending any time in jail. I'm proud of my bamboo fly rod and Weatherby rifle, having the friends I have, and hunting with my father and brother."

Philosophy of Life . . .

"Be happy, laugh a lot, and fish when possible. No matter how bad life may get, it's still good to be alive, so enjoy it as much as possible."

Ideal Woman . . .

"Someone who wants to spend time with me and has a good sense of humor. She has to be nice, enjoy the outdoors, fairly straight forward, no game players, no drugs or smoking, but drinking is OK. My ideal woman knows how to fly fish and hunt."

Paul's Lunch Menu

Fried Mushrooms
Tomato and Rice Soup
Milky Way Coffee

FRIED MUSHROOMS

– Serves 2

2 cups mushrooms
1 cup milk
1 cup flour
butter or margarine, as desired

1. Wash mushrooms and slice them in half.

2. Dip mushrooms in milk, then coat with flour.

3. In a large frying pan, heat some butter on medium-high heat. Add mushrooms and saute' until brown.

TOMATO AND RICE SOUP

– Serves 2

"It tastes good and it's easy to make."

1 can tomato soup
1 1/2 cups milk
1 medium tomato, diced
1/2 cup rice
1 teaspoon basil

1. Blend soup and milk in a sauce pan and bring to a boil.
2. Reduce heat and add rice. Cover with a lid and simmer until rice is soft.
3. A few minutes before serving, add basil and tomato. Serve with french bread.

MILKY WAY COFFEE

– Serves 2

"Great when it's cold or when you want to relax."

16 ounce cup of coffee or espresso
2 tablespoons chocolate syrup
1 tablespoon caramel syrup
sugar, to taste
cream, to taste
1 shot scotch whiskey, if cold out

1. Blend all ingredients together and enjoy.

TERRY

}
- Thirty Something
- Film and Video Production
- Ashland, Oregon

Hobbies and Interests . . .

"My hobbies and interests include attending swap meets and auctions. I like collecting art, old cameras, family home movies, and other collectibles. I enjoy watching old and new films and ballroom dancing—when I remember how! I like camping, hiking, live sports, playing volleyball, softball, lawn bowling, fishing, dancing, chess, and enjoying fine foods and drinks."

Goals . . .

"To create jobs, invent and produce motion pictures, market ideas, write movie scripts, and be successful, happy, and free. I want to implement a million dollar franchise business that would be a fun center for the whole family. I would like to help save the planet by legalizing hemp, exposing corrupt business people and politicians, helping the little

– continued next page

person, and creating a center for homeless children. I want to own and operate a motion picture/TV production facility, find my soulmate, partner, and have lots of babies."

Accomplishments . . .

"Earning Eagle Scout, becoming a U.S. Marine Corps expert shooter, working and paying my way through college to earn a B.S. in Broadcast Communications, being self-employed, a non-smoker, drug free, and an ultra-light drinker."

Philosophy of Life . . .

"Dare to be debt free. We must take responsibility for our actions and reactions. When you smile at a little child, you are doing something good. Do something good for someone else and don't tell anyone about it."

Ideal Woman . . .

"To be a 90's Donna Reed business person, spiritual but not a revelation extremist, an independent thinker, witty, open minded, successful, in shape but likes to eat. She should be willing to learn the waltz, be adventurous, rich in her heart, and romantic. Someone who has access to venture capitalists, investors and industrialists and is a good presenter."

Terry's Lunch Menu

Chicken Stoup
Cheese Bread
Rice Pudding

CHICKEN STOUP

– Serves 2

2 chicken legs

2 chicken thighs

6 stalks bok choy , chopped

6-8 leaves nappa cabbage, chopped

1 red onion, diced

4-5 celery stalks, chopped

2 or 3 eggs

garlic powder, to taste

salt, as desired

pepper, to taste

2 cups cooked rice

1. Fry chicken hot and fast for 10 to 12 minutes.
2. Fill a large pot with 2 quarts of water, bring to a boil. Add chicken and boil until done, about 20 minutes.
3. As water continues boiling, gradually add bok choy, cabbage, red onion, and celery.
4. Combine eggs, garlic, salt, and pepper then mix. Add to mixture in pot.
5. Reduce heat and simmer until vegetables are tender. Serve over cooked rice.

CHEESE BREAD

– Makes 6 servings

1 1/2 cups Bisquick
1/4 cup 2% milk
1 egg
1 cup grated sharp cheddar cheese
1 teaspoon poppy seeds
2 tablespoons margarine, melted

1. Combine Bisquick, milk, egg, and 1/2 of cheese. Stir just until moistened. Dough will be stiff and sticky.
2. Pat dough evenly onto slighty greased 9" pan. If dough is too sticky, flour your hands.
3. Sprinkle with remaining cheese and poppy seeds; pour melted margarine over the top.
4. Bake at 400° for 20 to 25 minutes or until golden brown.
5. Slice and serve hot.

RICE PUDDING
– Serves 4

"This is my Granny's recipe - she taught me how to make it this way."

2 cups cooked rice
3 cups milk
4 eggs
1/4 cup sugar
1 small box raisins
1 teaspoon vanilla
nutmeg, to taste

1. Combine all ingredients in a 5 x 9 glass pan (Pyrex)
2. Bake at 350° for 30 minutes or until custard sets.
3. Serve warm or chilled with cream or milk.

ROGER

- Thirty Something
- Producer/Actor/Makeup/Artist
- Eugene, Oregon

Hobbies and Interests . . .

"I'm kind of obsessed with collecting cars, clothes and Ming jars. I enjoy teaching what I have learned in life to young actors and actresses, hoping that some of my knowledge and experiences on stage and on screen will help them out in some way. I like most sports, water skiing, snow skiing, and music."

Goals . . .

"To have lots of exciting and interesting experiences! I like meeting new people, I'd like to travel around the world and I want to fall in love. Of course, I would like to be famous some day, but in the long run that really doesn't matter."

– continued next page

Accomplishments . . .

"I am proudest of the true friends I have met along the way including my two dogs, Ritsy and Bo Bo. I love them a lot and they make me laugh! I'm proud of my conviction to my career even through thick and thin...and sky diving, what a rush! What's yet to come..."

Philosophy of Life . . .

"To live each day to the fullest. To do unto others as I would have them do unto me. And, remember that life is never perfect, so be prepared for anything. Take nothing for granted because life is precious!"

Ideal Woman . . .

"Beauty, lots of heart and soul, humor and kindness. Age doesn't matter, or shape and size, as long as we are happy and compatible. She has to be sexy, too, and definitely like to play!"

Roger's Lunch Menu

Spinach Salad
Roger's Fantastic Quiche
Lemon Lush

SPINACH SALAD

– Serves 2

1 tomato, sliced into 6 sections	green olives, as desired
1 tablespoon Italian dressing	pepper, to taste
fresh spinach, enough for two salads	garlic salt, to taste
butter lettuce, enough for two salads	2 tablespoons of Worcestershire sauce
1 carrot, thinly sliced	juice of 1 lemon
1 celery stalk, sliced	sunflower seeds, as desired

1. Layer sliced tomatoes on 2 small salad plates. Pour Italian dressing over tomatoes.
2. Top with spinach, butter lettuce, carrots, celery and olives.
3. Sprinkle with pepper and garlic salt.
4. Add lemon juice and Worcestershire sauce.
5. Top with sunflower seeds.

ROGER'S FANTASTIC QUICHE ————————————————

– Makes 1 quiche

"I chose this fantastic quiche because it has heart and soul, and I can cook it! I have success with this dinner in the past."

1 large bakery fresh pie shell
mozzarella, Swiss and sharp Cheese,
   cubed, enough to fill 1 pie shell
1/2 cup sliced mushrooms
1/2 cup chopped broccoli
3 tablespoons lite cream cheese
3 eggs, beaten
3 tablespoons white wine

2 cups hot, non-fat milk
1 dash nutmeg
1 dash garlic
pepper, to taste
salt, to taste
Parmesan cheese, as desired
1 avocado, sliced
1 tomato, sliced

1. Fill pie shell with cubed cheeses. Add mushrooms and broccoli.
2. Mix cream cheese, eggs, white wine, milk, nutmeg, garlic, salt, and pepper. Pour over top of ingredients in pie shell.
3. Bake at 350° for 45 minutes or until firm.
4. Top with Parmesan cheese, avocado and tomatoes.

LEMON LUSH

1 cup flour

1 stick margarine

3/4 cup walnuts, chopped

1 8-ounce package lite cream cheese, room temperature

1 cup powdered sugar

1 9-ounce lite Cool Whip

2 small packages instant lemon pudding

3 cups 2% milk

Lemon Schnapps, as desired

1. Mix flour and margarine.
2. Add 1/2 cup of the nuts and press into a 9" x 13" pan. Bake at 350° for 15 minutes. Remove and cool.
3. With an electric mixer, beat cream cheese and powdered sugar. Fold in 1/2 tub of Cool Whip.
4. Pour into crust evenly.
5. Mix lemon pudding and milk. Beat until thick. Spread on top of cream cheese mixture.
6. Combine Lemon Schnapps and remaining Cool Whip, spread over pudding mixture.
7. Top with the remaining nuts and refrigerate before serving.

CHARLES

- Forty Something
- Writer
- Ashland, Oregon

Hobbies and Interests . . .

"My hobbies and interests include wood working (building and carving), reading, hiking, and environmental concerns, such as wildlife protection and reforestation."

Goals . . .

"My goals in life are simple. I continually strive to be a better human being, good to myself, other two-leggeds, and all living things. I plan to work with blind children, eventually, to bring them in touch with some of nature's finery. I also expect to finish my building projects, ranch endeavors, the barn, lake, and tree planting. On a more personal level, I am currently writing my second novel. I plan to finish it, and start on the third."

– continued next page

Accomplishments . . .

"The accomplishments I find most gratifying include: fathering and raising three healthy children, publishing my first novel, designing and constructing a home, and the fact that I have survived long enough to learn from my own mistakes."

Philosophy of Life . . .

"My philosophy of life is to take care of my own. To live and let live, with an eye to diversity, an ear to its song, and the patience to work at understanding human behavior."

Ideal Woman . . .

"My ideal woman is sound, honest, and loving. She walks equally well, alone, loving the five-leaf lupin, arms spread wide, faceup to the glory of giving light, mouth open, wanting more. She can move quietly, patiently, along the dark side of her mate, her presence an ember."

Charles' Lunch Menu

Mountain Machako
Lentil Soup with Ham Hocks

MOUNTAIN MACHAKO

– Serves 2

2 cloves garlic, minced

1/8 red or yellow onion, diced

1/2 pound venison or elk, cleaned, trimmed and thinly sliced

1 medium tomato, diced

1/2 2-ounce can jalapeno peppers

3 extra large eggs

1/2 4-ounce sour cream

1/2 dozen flour tortillas

1. Lightly oil a large skillet. Add garlic and onion. Simmer over low heat for 1 minute.

2. Add venison or elk. (Thinly sliced canned beef may be substituted.) Cook for 2 minutes on medium heat.

3. Add tomato and peppers. When mixture bubbles, reduce heat and simmer until most of the liquid is gone, stirring frequently.

4. In a medium bowl, lightly beat eggs. Add to the skillet and stir until eggs are cooked into the mixture.

5. Cover skillet and turn heat off.

6. Warm tortillas and spoon in Machako. Add sour cream to taste.

LENTIL SOUP WITH HAM HOCKS

"This is an easy meal that will simmer all day, and be appreciated when tired bones crawl back into camp."

> 3 tablespoons canola oil
> 6 cloves garlic, diced
> 1/2 onion, diced
> 4 cups water
> 1 teaspoon sweet basil
> 1/2 teaspoon salt
> 1/2 teaspoon cayenne pepper
> 1 bag lentils
> 4 ham hocks

1. In large pot, heat canola oil.
2. Add garlic and onion. When it begins to sizzle, add water and bring to a boil.
3. Add lentils, salt, cayenne, and basil. Stir over high heat until boiling.
4. Reduce heat to low, add ham hocks and cover.
5. Simmer for at least 3 hours.

MARK

- Forty Something
- Teacher
- Williams, Oregon

Hobbies and Interests . . .

"It's always fun to be on or in the water, take a hike, climb, play a game, etc., etc., etc. My other 'baggage' includes a need to travel. I've had the bug all my life and now I must run away several times a year. Whether it is Christmas in Jamaica, a drive up the Olympic Peninsula for a week, or a weekend in Tahoe...there is too much to see and do to stay home all the time. On the flip side, I can also be a homebody. I can go many days without leaving my address and keep myself busy with home projects and the sort. Quiet evenings at home relaxing are a must, and good movies a staple. Also, reading, eating good vegetarian food, country living with small doses of city fun, and concerts."

– continued next page

Goals . . .

"To try and improve myself as a person spiritually, intellectually, and physically. I know I am far from perfect, just ask anyone who knows me. Getting just one or two steps closer is a big goal. And, just as importantly, to have fun in life. In getting to that last goal, I have another one: To free myself from the system a little so I can live a more independent and liberated life."

Accomplishments . . .

"My accomplishments are very personal. The ones I will talk about include my education, professional achievements, and travels. I guess my greatest legacy of all is that I really enjoy life and try to spread it around a little."

Philosophy of Life . . .

"To have fun and enjoy my personal freedom. I believe that we are all connected and that all behavior we exhibit has a ripple effect on the universe. I am trying to give off positive ripples. I also believe that violence should be used last and only in self defense."

Ideal Woman . . .

"To be natural and simple. Also, she must enjoy my eccentricities, including my bizarre sense of humor. Of course, I want to be extremely attracted to her and she to me. She should want to take some chances and shake things up every once in a while. She should be part angel, but with a little devil, too! Passion and compassion are also very important to me."

Eggplant Parmesan
Mark's Garlic Bread

EGGPLANT PARMESAN

– Serves 4

"I chose this dinner because this was the first complete meal I learned to make back in college. I would impress all my first dates. They would think I was this great cook, but it was the only thing I knew how to make, so I could never invite them over for dinner again. Maybe that is why my love life never flourished in college?"

1 large eggplant, sliced into 1/8" slices, makes 20-25 slices	2 green peppers, sliced	black olives, sliced
2 tablespoons extra virgin olive oil	2-3 garlic cloves, chopped	1/4 cup cheddar cheese, grated
1/2 cup vegetable burger mix	1 large onion, chopped	1/4 cup Monteray Jack cheese, grated
1/2 cup whole wheat flour	10 mushrooms, sliced	1 small ricotta cheese
1 16-ounce jar of Classico or Newman's Own spaghetti sauce	1 yellow squash, sliced	
	1 tomato, diced	

1. In a bowl, combine burger mix and wheat flour together.
2. Dip eggplant in cold water, shake excess and dip in mixture. Cover completely.
3. In a large frying pan over medium heat, add oil to form a thin layer. Fry each battered eggplant slice for 3-4 minutes.
4. In a 9" x 13" dish, lightly oiled, add a thin layer of sauce, eggplant, then a second layer of sauce.
5. Layer 1/2 of all the vegetables and add a layer of ricotta cheese.
6. Sprinkle a layer of the two grated cheeses. Repeat process with sauce, eggplant, sauce, vegetables and cheeses. Save a little vegetables to add on top for color.
7. Bake in oven 30-40 minutes at 350°.

MARK'S GARLIC BREAD ————————————————

– Makes 1 loaf

1 loaf French bread
1/2 stick butter
3-4 garlic cloves, finely chopped

1. Split bread open through the center.
2. Spread with a thin layer of butter. Sprinkle garlic evenly throughout.
3. Wrap in tin foil and bake during the last 15 minutes with the eggplant. Unwrap slightly the last 2-3 minutes, if you prefer a crunchy garlic bread. Cut into 2" slices.

"For more romantic times, a bottle of wine goes very nicely. If you have room, invite Ben and Jerry over for dessert."

WILLIAM

} · **Fifty Something**
· **Stock and Commodity Trader**
· **Grants Pass, Oregon**

Hobbies and Interests . . .

"My hobbies and interests include the outdoors! I love the mountains and pristine high country. It is the main reason I moved here from the crowded east coast (Connecticut). I like fishing, hunting, gardening, and preparing exotic recipes."

Goals . . .

"To continue just like I am now. For me, I have reached the ultimate in locale, with a nice home and beautiful location in the country. I now would like to find someone nice to share it with me."

– continued next page

Accomplishments . . .

"The day I was designated a Naval Aviator with those 'magical wings of gold', and the time subsequent when I became a DC-8 Captain as an airline pilot are my proudest accomplishments."

Philosophy of Life . . .

"To be kind and considerate of others and to tolerate their occasional frailties, for I have enough of my own. I am a generous person and usually give more than I receive or expect in return, both materially and emotionally."

Ideal Woman . . .

"A lady who is kind and considerate, who is willing and likes to give as well as receive. Someone who likes the outdoors and camping, and who would savor the succulent aroma and taste of freshly cooked trout from a Coleman stove on the back of a pickup truck. Someone who likes candlelight dinners and fine cuisine. Someone willing to try new things with a 'spirit of adventure', and enjoys the Shakespeare Festival in Ashland."

William's Lunch Menu

**Amontillado Pheasant
Coshe
Moist Zucchini Bread**

AMONTILLADO PHEASANT

– Serves 2

"This is an exotic way to prepare wild upland game birds. It does not mask their natural flavor, but rather, enhances it."

1 pheasant (or 2 chukars)	1 garlic clove, minced
1 tablespoon butter	1/2 teaspoon salt
3/4 cup Amontillado sherry	1/2 teaspoon freshly ground
1/3 cup cooking oil	black pepper
juice of 1/2 lemon	1/4 teaspoon thyme
1/3 cup chopped onion	1/4 teaspoon marjoram

1. Quarter the bird by splitting the breast and legs.

2. Rub with butter and brown all sides over medium heat in a heavy frying pan.

3. Blend all remaining ingredients together and add to pan.

4. Simmer covered for 1 hour, or until meat is tender.

5. Serve over rice or cooked spaghetti.

COSHE

– Serves 4

"This is an old Lithuanian recipe passed down from my family for generations. A simple yet tasty use of potatoes, which was one of the staples of the poor peasants of the 'Old Country'."

5 potatoes, grated

1 medium onion, finely chopped

1 small can evaporated milk, undiluted

3 eggs, beaten

1 teaspoon salt

1/2 cup margarine, melted

1/3 cup flour

1. Combine all ingredients in any order except fold in the flour last.
2. Pour mixture into a 5 1/2" x 9 1/2" casserole baking dish.
3. Bake at 350° for 1 1/2 hours or until brown and crusty.

MOIST ZUCCHINI BREAD

– Yields 2 loaves

"This is the best zucchini bread I've ever tasted, and I have tasted many. It has crushed pineapple which gives it moisture and extra flavor, along with raisins."

3 eggs, beaten
1 cup oil
1 1/4 cups sugar
2 teaspoons vanilla
2 cups grated zucchini
1 8-ounce can crushed pineapple, drained
1 cup chopped walnuts

1/2 cup raisins
2 teaspoons baking soda
1 teaspoon salt
1/2 teaspoon baking powder
1 teaspoon cinnamon
3/4 teaspoon nutmeg
2 cups flour

1. Beat first four ingredients until thick and foamy.
2. Stir in zucchini and pineapple.
3. In a separate bowl combine dry ingredients, then add zucchini mixture and stir.
4. Fold in nuts and raisins.
5. Divide batter between 2 greased and floured 5 1/2" x 9 1/2" loaf pans.
6. Bake at 350° for 1 hour.
7. Slice and serve with butter or cream cheese. Bread can be frozen for future.

JEFF

}
- Forty Something
- Machinist
- Grants Pass, Oregon

Hobbies and Interests . . .

"I enjoy bow hunting, painting, drawing, working out, driving around, and visiting friends and family. I like going to movies and eating in nice restaurants. I am also working on an acting career and have made seven commercials and one video on child safety."

Goals . . .

"My goals in life are to become an accomplished actor and further my education in the psychology of human relations. I would also like to be married and have a family."

Accomplishments . . .

"Accomplishments I am proudest of are working with children in my third and fourth grade Sunday school class and learning how to hang glide."

– continued next page

Philosophy of Life . . .

"My philosophy of life is to honor your mother and father, respect God, have fun, play hard, be kind to others, and never give up."

Ideal Woman . . .

"She would be a woman with a teachable spirit, a good sense of humor, patience, and faithfulness. She would have a gentle spirit and a good work ethic."

Jeff's Lunch Menu

Japanese Consomme with Carrots
Tofu Salad
Stuffed Mushrooms

JAPANESE CONSOMME WITH CARROTS ───────────

– Serves 4-6

1 1/2 quarts water	soy sauce or sea salt, to taste
1-2 sheets konbu	1 carrot, sliced
3-5 shiitake mushrooms	1 teaspoon ginger juice
1/4 cup bonito flakes	1 scallion for garnish

1. In a large pot, bring water to a boil. Reduce heat and simmer konbu and mushrooms for 30 minutes to 1 hour or until konbu is tender.

2. Remove konbu and mushrooms, cut into strips, and set aside.

3. Add bonito flakes to hot water. When they sink to bottom, remove and discard flakes. Keep water.

4. Return konbu and mushrooms to pot. Season with soy sauce.

5. Add carrots. Simmer for 5 minutes. Add ginger juice. Garnish with scallions. Serve immediately.

Variations: Serve clear without konbu or mushrooms.
Add tiny tofu cubes or fresh, thinly sliced mushrooms.
To create a more decorative soup, cut carrots in shape of flowers.

TOFU SALAD

– Makes 2 sandwiches

1/4 pound firm tofu

1 1/2 tablespoons soy mayonnaise

1 tablespoon prepared mustard

1/4 green or red pepper, finely chopped

1 scallion, finely chopped

1 1/2 tablespoons pickle relish

1/2 tablespoon parsley, minced

optional: fresh dill, rosemary, thyme, and chives as desired

1. Rinse and drain tofu. Wrap in a towel and press out water.

2. Mash tofu to soft consistency with fork.

3. Mix the rest of the ingredients until smooth. Refrigerate until use.

JEFF'S STUFFED MUSHROOMS

– Serves 4

"Stuffed mushrooms make a good appetizer. It is a favorite of mine because I have always liked the smell and taste of mushrooms."

12 mushrooms, brushed clean

3 ounces cream cheese

1/4 cup butter, melted

1/8 teaspoon garlic salt

1. Remove mushroom stems and fill with cream cheese.
2. Mix butter and garlic salt, pour over top of mushrooms.
3. Bake at 350° until cheese has melted and slightly browned.

TOM

- Fifty Something
- Retail Clerk
- Portland, Oregon

Hobbies and Interests . . .

"I enjoy gardening, driving my TR-6 on sunny days, cooking, and deep sea fishing."

Goals . . .

"To have a full life, see Europe and the world, enjoy my life, be active, see the sunrises, and sunsets."

Accomplishments . . .

"I raised two daughters after my divorce and cared for my aging father. I re-entered college and finished with a B.A. from George Fox College in 1991."

– continued next page

Philosophy of Life . . .

"What you put out you will get back. Life is a wonderful thing if you just take time to enjoy it."

Ideal Woman . . .

"She must be outgoing and friendly, sincere, and honest. She is someone with style and grace who appreciates good food and fine wine."

Tom's Lunch Menu

Tex-Mex Jumbo Prawns
Cold Gazpacho Soup
Melon Wraps

TEX-MEX JUMBO PRAWNS

– Serves 2

8 - 12 jumbo prawns

2/3 cup olive oil

1/2 package taco seasoning mix

2 ears of fresh corn, kernels removed from cob

1/2 red bell pepper, sliced

1/2 yellow bell pepper, sliced

1 package of favorite rice dish

chicken stock

fresh cilantro or green onion, chopped

1. Shell and devein prawns, leaving the last shell section and tail attached. Butterfly and set aside.

2. Using an electric fry pan or skillet, heat olive oil and taco seasoning on medium-high. Add prawns and lightly saute´.

3. Add red peppers, yellow peppers, and corn to prawns. Toss together and heat thoroughly.

4. Cook your favorite rice according to package instructions, substituting chicken stock for water.

5. Warm a platter, add rice, top with prawns and vegetables. Garnish with chopped cilantro or green onion, and serve with heated tortillas.

COLD GAZPACHO SOUP

– *Serves 2*

1 16-ounce can clamato juice

1/2 cucumber

1/2 yellow bell pepper

1/2 red bell pepper

1 large ripe tomato, peeled

3 dashes Tabasco

2 teaspoons balsamic vinegar

2 teaspoons chopped fresh garlic

sour cream, as desired

fresh cilantro for garnish

1. Using a food processor, blend all ingredients, except sour cream and cilantro, until smooth.

2. Chill 24 hours before serving.

3. At time of serving, place soup in shallow bowls. Top with a small amount of sour cream that has been blended with a dash or two of Tabasco and place fresh cilantro leaves in sour cream.

MELON WRAPS
– Yields 12 wedges

1 honeydew melon
12 slices New York sharp cheddar cheese
12 thin slices Prosciutto ham

1. Cut melon in half, removing the seeds and rind.
2. Slice melon into 12 wedges.
3. Place a slice of cheese on each melon wedge.
4. Wrap a slice of Prosciutto ham around the melon and cheese wedge.

Variation: substitute your favorite melon for honeydew.

SECTION THREE

Dinner
Bachelors

JEROME

- Thirty Something
- Pipefitter
- Portland, Oregon

Hobbies and Interests . . .

"I enjoy weight lifting, mountain biking, rollerblading, and basketball. I also like to hunt, fish, camp, and just be out of doors. Cooking is a big hobby of mine. I like music and reading."

Goals . . .

"To be the best father I can be is the most important goal at this point in my life.
Other goals are to stay fit and never lose the 'kid' in me. I want my own house and be able to build on my retirement funds, so I can have fun when I retire."

Accomplishments . . .

"The effort I put into being the best dad I am has paid off a hundred times over. I am proud of going from an overweight 34 year old to a very fit 37 year old. My other accomplishments are not as meaningful as they used to be."

– continued next page

Philosophy of Life . . .

"Always treat people just like you would want to be treated. Always give your best effort when you do anything. Work hard and be positive so positive things will happen in your life. Laugh as much as possible, because it is good for the soul."

Ideal Woman . . .

"She would be fit and outgoing with a big heart. She would enjoy the outdoors and have a great sense of humor."

Barbecued Teriyaki Salmon
Parmesan Zucchini

BARBECUED TERIYAKI SALMON

– Serves 2

"I have so many favorites it's hard to choose just one. This one was chosen because most people like salmon over other seafoods. The teriyaki gives the salmon a very different flavor, I'm sure you will love."

1 pound salmon fillets, unskinned	1 teaspoon garlic powder
Marinara Sauce:	1/2 teaspoon ground ginger
1/2 cup soy sauce	1/8 teaspoon pepper
1/4 cup vegetable oil	2 tablespoons sugar
1 1/2 teaspoon ground mustard	1 stalk green onion, chopped

1. Mix soy sauce and vegetable oil then add the rest of the ingredients in any order. Mix well. This is the marinara.

2. Marinate salmon in a sealed container or reclosable baggy for 24-36 hours.

3. Place skinless side of salmon over hot coals for 5 minutes.

4. Flip salmon to opposite, skinned side, for 20 minutes. Cover with lid. Cooking time will vary with personal preference.

PARMESAN ZUCCHINI
– *Serves 2*

3 large garlic cloves, finely chopped

1/2 cup onions, chopped

1 teaspoon vegetable oil

2 to 3 zucchini squash, cut in 1/4 " slices

1/2 jalapeno pepper, chopped with seeds removed

1/2 cup red pepper, chopped

1/2 cup yellow pepper, chopped

1 14 1/2-ounce can stewed tomatoes

1/2 cup fresh ground Parmesan cheese

1. Saute' garlic and onions in vegetable oil over medium-high heat until soft.
2. Add zucchini and peppers and saute' until zucchini starts to soften. Add tomatoes.
3. Simmer until zucchini is done and add 1/4 cup of the Parmesan cheese. Keep covered until ready to eat.
4. Add remaining cheese just before serving.

DOUG

- Thirty Something
- Food Service Manager
- Eagle Creek, Oregon

Hobbies and Interests . . .

"My hobbies and interests include cooking, playing the guitar, spelunking (cave exploring), hiking, camping, fishing, gardening, and bicycling. One of my current interests is computer literacy, from which I hope to obtain more information through the internet, as well as organize recipes and inventory control at work."

Goals . . .

"Besides providing my son with a decent upbringing, my goals in life are to gain more knowledge and skills that I can utilize in my profession. At the same time I'd like to enjoy life, hopefully with someone who has similar interests, enjoying the many treasures life has to offer."

– continued next page

Accomplishments . . .

"The accomplishments I'm proudest of are being fortunate to have raised such a good kid that I'd obtained sole custody of prior to his 1st birthday. He really enjoys outings with his dad. Other accomplishments I'm proud of are to have used a bicycle for sole transportation for 13 years, year round, the skills and knowledge of food I learned through my 18 years cooking, including a three year chef's apprenticeship program and teaching myself to play guitar."

Philosophy of Life . . .

"You get out of life what you put into it. Hard work pays off. Always try to be fair and treat people how you'd like to be treated. Enjoy life while you're here, cause you're just passin' through, and if you're going to do it, do it right or don't do it at all!"

Ideal Woman . . .

"The qualities my ideal woman would have are being faithful, understanding, having a good sense of humor, full of energy and a desire for fun. Having patience and compassion for children are also important, as well as compatibility with her mate and a passion for romance."

Doug's Dinner Menu

Spinach Salad with Hot Bacon Dressing
Scallop and Prawns "Flavious"
Focaccia
Hazelnut Cheesecake with Huckleberry Sauce

SPINACH SALAD WITH HOT BACON DRESSING ———————

– Serves 2

"This is my favorite way of preparing spinach for a salad. You don't have the crispness of the spinach leaves as when it's served cold, but I think the hot bacon dressing brings out the flavor of the spinach."

4 cups spinach, washed, and blotted dry
1 hard cooked egg, finely chopped
2 tablespoons finely diced onion
2 strips thick bacon
1 tablespoons olive oil
1/4 cup chicken stock
1 tablespoon red wine vinegar
1 medium garlic clove, finely chopped
1/4 teaspoon curry powder

1. Toss the spinach with egg and onion, thoroughly coating all the leaves with the hard cooked egg yolk.
2. Cook the bacon until crisp. Remove bacon and set aside. Reserve about 1 tablespoon of the grease. Add remaining ingredients to the grease and bring to a boil. Pour over spinach, gently mixing.
3. Garnish with chopped, crisp bacon.

SCALLOP AND PRAWNS "FLAVIOUS"

For marinara sauce:

– Yields 1 1/2 cups

1 1/2 tablespoons olive oil

3 cloves garlic, peeled and finely diced

2 tablespoons finely diced onion

1 cup fresh or canned tomato, peeled and diced

1/4 cup chicken stock

1 tablespoon chopped dried basil leaves

1/4 cup tomato sauce

1. Saute' garlic and onion in olive oil on medium heat for approximately 5 minutes.
2. Reduce heat to medium-low. Add tomatoes and basil, cook 5 more minutes.
3. Add tomato sauce and chicken stock. Simmer for 10 to 15 minutes.

For the pasta:

4 ounces linguine pasta, uncooked

4-5 ounces bay scallops

4-5 ounces prawns, peeled and deveined

1/2 shallot, peeled and finely diced

1 1/2 tablespoons olive oil

1/8 cup white wine, preferably Reisling

1/8 cup heavy cream, room temperature

1/8 cup fresh grated Parmesan cheese

2 sprigs fresh basil leaves

1. Cook pasta in lightly salted, boiling water until al dente. Drain, then rinse with cold water.
2. Saute' scallops and prawns with shallots in olive oil on medium-high heat for about 3 minutes or until scallops turn opaque and the prawns bright orange and white.
3. Add white wine, reduce for 1 minute.
4. Add marinara sauce and heavy cream. Simmer 2 to 3 minutes.
5. Re-heat pasta by dipping it into boiling water, then drain.
6. Arrange pasta on plates and evenly distribute the seafood and sauce. Sprinkle with Parmesan and garnish with fresh basil.

FOCACCIA

– Yields 1 10" wheel

Use a scale to weigh the ingredients.

1 pound and 1 ounce bread flour

1/2 ounce sugar

1/2 ounce salt

1/2 ounce olive oil

3/4 ounce yeast

10 ounces water, under 110°F

1/4 cup total fresh herbs;

garlic, oregano, basil, thyme, and parsley

For the crust finish:

1/8 cup olive oil

2 tablespoons grated Parmesan cheese

1. Knead the above ingredients (except the crust finish), together in a mixer with a dough hook for 10 minutes.
2. Roll dough out into a 12" circular shape and place in a lightly floured 12" cake pan.
3. Brush 1/8 cup olive oil over the top and sprinkle about 2 tablespoons Parmesan cheese.
4. Proof at 110° until double in volume.
5. Bake at 450° for 15 to 20 minutes until crisp and brown on top.
6. Cut into wedges.

HAZELNUT CHEESECAKE WITH HUCKLEBERRY SAUCE

– Yields 1 9" cake

2 1/2 cups graham cracker crumbs
1/2 cup powdered sugar
1/2 cup butter
2 1/2 pounds cream cheese
1 3/4 cups sugar
1/4 cup flour
1/2 teaspoon almond extract

4 eggs, beaten
2 egg yolks
1/4 cup whipping cream
1/4 cup hazelnuts, roasted,
    peeled and finely chopped
non-stick cooking spray

1. Thoroughly spray a 9" spring form pan with non-stick cooking spray.

2. Mix graham cracker crumbs and sugar in a bowl, then cut in butter. Reserve 1/4 cup for topping. Press tightly into pan.

3. Combine cream cheese, sugar, flour and extract. Beat until smooth and fluffy.

4. Add eggs and egg yolks 1/3 at a time, beating after each addition.

5. Blend in cream and add hazelnuts.

6. Pour mixture into pan and sprinkle reserved graham cracker crumbs over the top.

7. Bake at 250° for 2 hours. Turn oven off and let stand 1 hour in oven.

8. Refrigerate overnight on wire rack for cooling. Remove from pan to serve.

"Cooking is a great way for me to relieve stress and be creative!"

HUCKLEBERRY SAUCE
– Yields 3 cups

2 cups huckleberries, washed and stemmed
1/2 cup orange juice
1/2 cup sugar
1 ounce Kirsh (cherry brandy)
3 tablespoons cornstarch
1/4 cup water
fresh mint sprigs

1. Cook huckleberries in orange juice, sugar, and Kirsh on medium-high heat for about 20 minutes.
2. Mix cornstarch with water and slowly add to huckleberries, stirring until desired thickness.
3. Chill, then serve over hazelnut cheesecake.
4. Garnish with mint.

JERRY

- Thirty Something
- Self Employed
- Talent, Oregon

Hobbies and Interests . . .

"My hobbies and interests include running, bicycling, weight training, dancing, reading, movies, music, and sports."

Goals . . .

"I want to travel around the world at least once, attain financial independence and security, fish for halibut in Alaska, write a story for 'Chicken Soup for the Soul', earn a diploma to be a nutritional consultant, establish a student-athlete scholarship in my name, own a computer and printer, be happily married, raise $1 million for a cause or charity, and learn to water ski and snow ski."

– continued next page

Accomplishments . . .

"I am proudest of earning my bachelors degree, learning how to dance, building a profitable small business, enhancing my personal appearance and self esteem, achieving debt-free status, and my recognition in athletics."

Philosophy of Life . . .

"Life is a competition with myself... to do and be the best I can for myself, my family, my community, and the world."

Ideal Woman . . .

"My ideal woman has honesty, faithfulness, beauty—physical and spiritual, integrity, humor, persistence. She is hard-working, intelligent, goal oriented, concerned for people, forgiving, adventurous, loving, understanding, and she has a desire to learn."

Honey and Orange Chicken
Honey Mustard Vegetables

"These recipes were chosen because they are Satisfying, Healthy, and Easy to prepare. Hence, I am entitling this my S.H.E. dinner."

HONEY AND ORANGE CHICKEN

– Serves 4

1/4 cup frozen orange juice concentrate

3 tablespoons honey

1 tablespoon lemon juice

1/2 teaspoon finely grated orange peel

1/2 teaspoon ginger

4 chicken breast

orange marmalade

orange slices

1. In a baking dish, mix together orange juice concentrate, 2 tablespoons honey, lemon juice, orange peel and ginger. Add chicken pieces, coating all sides. Marinate for 10 minutes.

2. Bake uncovered at 400° for 8 minutes. Baste with pan juices. Bake 8 more minutes and baste.

3. Mix marmalade and remaining honey then glaze chicken. Bake approximately 10 minutes or until no pink remains.

4. Transfer chicken to serving plate. Reduce pan juices until thickened then pour over chicken. Garnish with orange slices.

HONEY MUSTARD VEGETABLES

– Serves 4

"I guarantee the daring woman who calls will not only find the dinner to be above and beyond her expectations, but the company to be even better!"

> 1/2 cup thinly sliced carrots
> 1/4 cup chopped brocolli
> 1/4 cup chopped cauliflower
> 2 tablespoons Dijon mustard
> 1/2 teaspoon dill weed
> 2 tablespoons honey

1. Steam carrots for 10 minutes.

2. Add brocolli and cauliflower and steam until tender.

3. Combine mustard, dill, and honey until smooth. Add to hot vegetables and stir until evenly coated with mustard mixture.

DAVID

> · **Fifty Something**
> · **Real Estate Lawyer**
> · **Portland, Oregon**

Hobbies and Interests . . .

"My hobbies and interests include cooking, music (playing the guitar and singing blues, country and rock n' roll), training bird dogs, boating and fishing, and collecting (books, antiques, art, and guitars)."

Goals . . .

"Lead a balanced life with time for professional growth, family, public service and pursuit of my own interests. To have fun!"

Accomplishments . . .

"I am proudest of raising two great kids! I have received awards for professional accomplishments. I am proud to have led a balanced life so as to accomplish the above and still have a rewarding personal life."

– continued next page

Philosophy of Life . . .

"Whatever you do, do it well, and be fair and kind in dealings with others. Life always involves some struggles, but if you look at the bright side and maintain a sense of humor it will be fun."

Ideal Woman . . .

"Good sense of humor, reasonably attractive, intelligent, good character, good communication skills, compatible interests and irreverent approach to life."

David's Dinner Menu

Barbecued Salmon
Sauted Green Beans
Grilled Corn on the Cob
Garlic Bread

BARBECUED SALMON ─────────────

– Serves 2

"This is the greatest! ...The fish tastes like barbecued steak. This is the best barbecued salmon I've found. Try it!"

1 salmon
margarine or butter, as desired
Lawry's seasoning salt, to taste

1. Filet or cut fish in half.

2. Spread margarine on flesh and sprinkle heavily with seasoning salt.

3. Place flesh side down on grill and cover immediately to avoid flare-ups. Coals should be gray with medium heat. (Note: this recipe is designed to be done on a charcoal barbecue with a tight fitting cover such as a Weber. If using a gas barbecue, the fish should be cooked with the skin side down for two-thirds of the cooking time and turned over for the final third.)

4. Cook for 5 to 20 minutes depending on heat of fire and thickness of fish.

5. Turn and cook skin-side down until white grease oozes out of flesh.

SAUTED GREEN BEANS —————————————————

– Serves 2

> 1/2 pound fresh green beans
> olive oil
> 1 clove garlic, minced
> salt, to taste
> pepper, to taste

1. Cut tips off green beans and boil in salted water for about 8 minutes. Drain.
2. Saute green beans in a skillet with just enough olive oil to cover the bottom of the pan. Add garlic. Saute for about 5 minutes, stirring regularly.
3. Add salt and pepper to taste.

GRILLED CORN ON THE COB
– Serves 2

1 or 2 ears fresh corn per person, with husks

butter, as desired

salt, to taste

1. Place ears of corn, with husks still attached, on barbecue grill at medium-hot temperature.
2. Grill for about 15 minutes, turning corn several times.
3. When husks are a little charred around the edges, the corn should be done. Don't worry if the corn itself is a little bit charred, as this only adds flavor.
4. To eat, peel back the husks and strip away the corn silk. The peeled away husks make handy handles for holding onto the ears of corn, or else can be cut off with a chef's knife.
5. Garnish with butter and salt if desired.

123

DAVID'S GARLIC BREAD

– Makes 1 loaf

> 1 loaf French bread
> butter or margarine
> garlic salt, to taste
> paprika, to taste
> Italian seasoning, to taste

1. Slice French bread in half, length-wise. Cover it with a generous coating of butter or margarine.
2. Sprinkle with salt, paprika, and Italian seasoning for flavor and visual appeal.
3. Broil for about 7 minutes, keeping a close watch on the bread, as once it starts to brown it gets done very quickly and can easily be overcooked.

JR

- Thirty Something
- Manager
- Medford, Oregon

Hobbies and Interests . . .

"When I feel the desire to relax, I often find myself hiking in the mountains of Southern Oregon, enjoying the scenery, and capturing the views and subtleties on black and white film. I strive to enjoy the things around me, the items most individuals take for granted. I may also be found walking the fairways of the nearest golf course. I find golf provides me with an opportunity to enjoy a sport which can be played in most any area I visit, and allows me the ability to meet interesting people."

Goals . . .

"I find myself striving to enjoy the people around me on a daily basis. My career is important to me because through this, I am able to experience opportunities others may only dream of. After meeting the woman who can balance out my life, I want to spend time enjoying her company. When the time is right, building a close family together would help me realize a few of my main goals in life."

– continued next page

Accomplishments . . .

"By achieving the quality of life I have at this time, creating the friendships I have, succeeding in my chosen career, and being able to hold my nose at a friendly level, I feel as though I have met some of the most important accomplishments I have set out to achieve."

Philosophy of Life . . .

" To simply state my philosophy of life:

Before I was here,
The sun still rose.

Long after I am gone,
The rivers will continue to flow.

But as long as I am on this earth,
The beauty is mine to enjoy,
As long as I remember to take the time."

Ideal Woman . . .

"The beauty of women is that each one is different. To expect a female to be extracted from a mold, would destroy the sheer beauty of this. To think a woman could be as simple as a recipe, would only show a naivete' in understanding her true beauty. I find intelligence and the ability to enjoy life, qualities of importance, in order for a woman to be satisfied with herself. Once this is accomplished and combined with a sincere caring for those around her, a woman's beauty has only begun to blossom."

**Spaghetti Carbonara
Mushrooms and Wine Sauce
Apple Raisin Quiche**

SPAGHETTI CARBONARA

– Serves 2

3 slices bacon, diced

1/4 cup dry white wine

1 extra large egg, room temperature

1/3 cup grated Parmesan cheese

6 ounces uncooked spaghetti (1 small package is 12 ounces)

pepper, to taste

1. In a skillet, lightly saute' bacon, do not brown. Add white wine and cook liquid down. Set aside, but keep warm.
2. Beat eggs slightly, add cheese and bacon, then blend. Reserve bacon grease.
3. Cook spaghetti and drain.
4. Add the hot bacon grease to the spaghetti then quickly add the egg and cheese mixture so that the hot grease will cook the eggs.
5. Toss with black pepper and serve immediately.

MUSHROOMS AND WINE SAUCE

– *Serves 2*

1/2 pound fresh mushrooms, washed and halved

1 medium green bell pepper, cut in 1 inch pieces

1/2 medium onion, coarsely chopped

1/4 cup margarine

1/2 teaspoon minced garlic

1 tablespoon Dijon mustard

1/4 cup brown sugar

1 tablespoon Worcestershire sauce

1/4 cup plus 2 tablespoons mellow red wine

pepper, to taste

1. Melt margarine and saute' onions until transparent.
2. Add mushrooms and peppers to onions and saute' for 10 to 15 minutes, stirring often.
3. Blend together mustard, brown sugar and Worcestershire sauce until smooth. Add the wine and pepper; stir well.
4. When mushrooms begin to brown and shrink, add the wine sauce.
5. Simmer for 45 minutes or until sauce is much reduced and thickened, mushrooms and peppers will be very dark.

APPLE RAISIN QUICHE

– Makes 1 10" quiche

"The only items to accompany this dish should be a cup of gourmet coffee and plenty of light-hearted conversation."

1 10" unbaked pie shell
1/4 cup raisins
3 large apples, peeled, cored and thinly sliced
1 cup whipping cream
2 eggs
1/2 cup sugar
1 teaspoon ground cinnamon

1. Heat oven to 475°. Bake the pie shell until lightly golden.
2. Sprinkle raisins into the bottom of the pie shell; top with apples.
3. In a large mixing bowl, combine cream, eggs, sugar, and cinnamon. Pour over apples.
4. Bake for 10 minutes, then reduce heat to 350° and bake an additional 50 minutes, or until set.

STEPHEN

- Thirty Something
- Executive Chef
- Talent, Oregon

Hobbies and Interests . . .

"I have been playing drums in bands since age 16. I currently play in a local band. I enjoy mountain bike riding, camping on the coast, golf and bowling. I have raised a baby iguana, which is now close to five feet in length! "Spider", my basset hound dog, commands a lot of attention and is very important to me."

Goals . . .

"I have been very goal oriented over the years, and have completed many of them. I have a great job, own my own house, car, etc. My goal now is to meet a nice woman and set new goals. Raising a family is first and foremost."

– continued next page

Accomplishments . . .

"Being appointed as corporate executive chef of a large hotel chain at age 28. I opened my own restaurant in 1990 which was a challenge and a success. My newest accomplishment as chef for Rogue Valley Country Club is my proudest to date."

Philosophy of Life . . .

"Learning from my past mistakes. Treating others as you want to be treated, and never take anything too seriously. I always look for a way to beat the system in which we live. I believe in God and what goes around comes around!"

Ideal Woman . . .

"Petite, cute, secure, and understanding. She is patient and not controlling, stable, and confident. She has a sense of adventure and a sense of humor. Someone who respects and loves me no matter what."

Dungeness Crab Pancakes with Saffron Sauce
Warm Duck Salad with Raspberry Vinegar and Peppered Bacon
Roast Rack of Lamb with Mint Pesto Crust
Texas Chocolate Massacre

DUNGENESS CRAB PANCAKES WITH SAFFRON SAUCE

– Serves 2

"I love fresh Dungeness crab. It reminds me of the walks on the beaches of the Oregon coast, the smell of a roaring campfire at night, and the laughter and wonder as we lower those poor creatures into the boiling water."

For the crab pancakes:

6 ounces Dungeness crab meat	1 pinch sea salt
2 tablespoons mayonnaise	1 pinch paprika
1 tablespoon fresh sliced basil	1 dash Tabasco
1 tablespoon finely diced onion	1 pinch ground black pepper
1 tablespoon finely diced green pepper	4 tablespoons bread crumbs
1 dash lemon juice	1 ounce olive oil
1 egg, beaten	2 fresh dill sprigs (garnish)

1. Clean shell fragments, if any, from the crab meat.
2. Mix mayonnaise, basil, onion, green pepper, lemon juice, egg, salt, paprika, Tabasco, and black pepper in a mixing bowl.
3. Fold in crab meat and bread crumbs. Shape into two patties about 3/4" thick, 4" round.
4. Heat the olive oil in a cast iron skillet over medium heat. Brown the pancakes on each side, remove onto paper towels; set aside.
5. Serve with Saffron Sauce and garnish with dill.   *(see next page for sauce)*

SAFFRON SAUCE ———————————————————

1 shallot, finely diced
1 tablespoon olive oil
1 ounce brandy
1 pinch saffron
1 tablespoon pink peppercorn
1/2 pint heavy cream
1 1/2 tablespoons whole butter
sea salt, to taste
1 pinch ground white pepper

1. In a heavy sauce pan heat olive oil. Add shallot and saute' until translucent.
2. Add saffron and brandy then stir. Reduce brandy by one half.
3. Add cream and simmer over low heat for 5 minutes or until it begins to thicken.
4. Add pink peppercorns and whip in butter gradually. Season with salt and white pepper.
5. Reheat the crab pancakes in a 350° oven for 5 minutes.
6. Ladle 2 ounces of the sauce into the center of two 9" plates. Place the crab pancakes on top of the sauce. Garnish with fresh dill sprigs.

WARM DUCK SALAD
WITH RASPBERRY VINEGAR AND PEPPERED BACON

– Serves 2

"With winter approaching, our elusive feathered friends are fleeing south. Before they get away, try this dish. It is one of my favorite specialties."

1 6-8 ounce duck breast, with skin	**For the dressing:**	6 mushrooms, sliced
	2 ounces pepper bacon, diced	1 ounce raspberry vinegar
1 bunch baby spinach leaves	1 tablespoon brown sugar	1 ounce brandy
	1 tablespoon Dijon mustard	3 ounces chicken broth
1 tablespoon toasted sesame seeds	1 shallot, diced	sea salt, to taste
	1 teaspoon chopped fresh garlic	pepper, to taste

1. Heat a cast iron skillet over medium-high heat. Sear the duck breast, skin side down, to withdraw the natural grease. Turn and brown the other side until medium to medium rare. Set aside on a paper towel.

2. In the same pan, pour off the grease from the duck and saute' the bacon until crisp.

3. Pour off 1/2 the fat from the bacon, then add the shallots and garlic, saute' for 1 minute.

4. Add the mushrooms, stir, and saute' until the mushrooms are tender.

5. Flame with brandy, reduce for 1 minute. (Note: Flaming brandy is done on a gas stove only. To flame brandy remove the skillet from the flame, add the brandy, return the skillet to the flame and shake, the brandy will catch. If using an electric burner skip the flaming step. Pour the brandy into the skillet and reduce.)

6. Add vinegar. Stir in the mustard and brown sugar, add the chicken stock, reduce until dressing thickens slightly. Season with salt and pepper, if needed.

7. Arrange spinach leaves on salad plates. Thinly slice the duck breast and place on top of spinach. Ladle on the warm dressing and sprinkle with sesame seeds.

ROAST RACK OF LAMB WITH MINT PESTO CRUST

– Serves 2

"The unmistakable aroma of lamb roasting in the oven and a candlelit room, should warm any girl's heart, especially served with a glass of rich red wine."

For the lamb:
- farm raised domestic rack of lamb, split saddle
- 1 ounce olive oil
- sea salt and ground black pepper, to taste

For the crust:
- 1/4 stick whole butter
- 2 slices white bread, crust removed
- 3 tablespoons fresh mint leaves
- 2 tablespoons toasted pine nuts
- 1 teaspoon chopped fresh garlic
- 1 1/2 teaspoons olive oil
- 3 tablespoons grated Parmesan cheese
- 1/2 ounce green creme de menthe

1. Place the butter, bread, mint leaves, and pine nuts in food processor. Press pulse button and combine until smooth.
2. Add the garlic and slowly drizzle in olive oil and creme de menthe while processor is running.
3. Mix in the Parmesan cheese.
4. Remove mixture to another container and set aside.

For the lamb:

1. In a heavy skillet heat 1 ounce olive oil.
2. Rub the "eye" or meat of the lamb with a little salt and pepper. Sear on all sides of meat until brown, remove and let cool.
3. Pack the pesto crust around the seared meat about 1/8" thick on all sides. Place in skillet and roast in 350° oven for 15 to 20 minutes, or until an internal temperature of 120°.
4. Remove from oven and let rest for 5 minutes.
5. Using a sharp knife, slice between the bones to produce lamb chops. Fan three of each onto warmed dinner plates. Serve with steamed asparagus and roasted potatoes.

TEXAS CHOCOLATE MASSACRE

– Serves 2

"Don't be afraid...it's only food. This dessert is basically a parfait. The presentation though is both dramatic and intriguing. Venture forth...this is my signature dessert dish."

For the chocolate mousse:

4 ounces cream cheese, softened
1/2 cup powdered sugar
1/2 teaspoon vanilla extract

1/4 cup Baker's sweet cocoa
2 cups heavy whipping cream

1. Cream together the cream cheese, powdered sugar, vanilla and cocoa.
2. Whip the cream separately until it holds a peak. Fold into cream mixture. Place into a pastry bag without a tip; set aside.

For the chocolate cake:

3 1/2 cups unbleached flour
2 tablespoons baking powder
3/4 cup cocoa
1 cup butter, softened

2 cups sugar
1 1/2 teaspoons vanilla extract
2 cups milk
4 egg whites

1. Mix together the flour, baking powder, and cocoa in a stainless steel bowl.
2. Combine butter, 1 cup of the sugar, vanilla, and milk, mix well.
3. Add the sugar mixture into the flour mixture.
4. Beat the egg whites with the remaining 1 cup of sugar until frothy. Add to the cake mixture, stir until smooth.
5. Pour and spread evenly onto a buttered and floured 12" x 18" sheet pan. Bake at 350° for about 30 minutes. Remove from oven and let cool.

(continues next page)

For the final touch:

1 pint strawberries, sliced

2 tablespoon sugar

1 tablespoon brandy

1 cup heavy whipping cream

1 cup dark sweet chocolate

1. Mix the strawberries, 1 tablespoon of sugar and brandy; set aside.
2. Whip whipping cream and remaining sugar together until the cream holds soft peaks.

——— To assemble the Massacre: ———

1. Cut baking parchment paper into two 3" x 12" strips. Bend into 3 1/2" rings and tape to hold the shape. Place the paper rings on a plate, side by side.
2. With a 3 1/2" round cookie cutter, cut 2 round pieces from the cake. Lift out carefully and lower cake into the paper rings. Push down gently to form the base.
3. Pipe about 2 or 3 ounces of the mousse on top of the cake, about 1" thick.
4. Top with some of the strawberries, pushing lightly into the mousse.
5. Spoon the whipped cream over the strawberries, about 1/2" thick. Place in freezer to set, about 30 minutes, or until firm.
6. Melt dark sweet chocolate over a double boiler. Pour melted chocolate onto a sheet pan covered with parchment paper. Spread out thin with a rubber spatula. Place in freezer to set up hard.
7. Remove the parfaits from the freezer and carefully peel the paper off. Using a spatula, lift each onto the center of a dessert plate.
8. Break off 4" tall pieces of the hardened chocolate, stick two into each of the massacres, to form a winglike appearance. May be served with fruit puree or creme anglaise around the dessert, if desired.

DAVID

- Thirty Something
- Wood Worker
- Grants Pass, Oregon

Hobbies and Interests . . .

"My hobbies include camping, photography and video making. I enjoy playing tennis, golfing, bowling, and playing basketball. I like going to concerts such as Amy Grant, Whitney Houston, Fleetwood Mac, and Heart. I also like going to movies, ball games, and dancing."

Goals . . .

"To always be happy and live a good life. To find a good woman to marry, buy a new home together, and travel wherever we would like to go."

– continued next page

Accomplishments . . .

"I am proudest of buying my first condo in 1980, in Redmond, Washington and buying a condo in Grants Pass back in 1987, where I still live."

Philosophy of Life . . .

"To be honest and hard working. Trust in God and enjoy life."

Ideal Woman . . .

"My ideal woman is nice, fun to be with, and honest."

David's Dinner Menu

Blue Cheese Salad and Mustard Chive Dressing
Apple and Green Pepper Pork Chops
Simple Potato Casserole
Strawberry Pie

BLUE CHEESE SALAD AND MUSTARD CHIVE DRESSING ————

– Serves 2

1/2 head romaine lettuce

1/2 cup cherry tomatoes, halved

1/4 cup blue cheese, crumbled

1/4 cup well drained, julienne-cut beets

4 tablespoons finely chopped parsley

1. Rinse, drain, and trim core from lettuce.

2. Tear into bite size pieces (you should have about 4 cups).

3. Just before serving, mix lettuce and cherry tomatoes. Toss lightly with Chive Dressing.

4. Top with cheese, beets, and parsley.

<u>Mustard Chive Dressing</u>

– Yields 1/2 cup

1/4 cup vegetable oil

2 tablespoons red wine vinegar

2 tablespoons olive oil

1 pinch salt

1 teaspoon Dijon mustard

1 dash pepper

2 tablespoons finely chopped chives

1. In blender or food processor combine salad oil, red wine vinegar, olive oil, salt, Dijon mustard, pepper, and chives.

2. Process until smoothly blended. If dressing is made ahead, shake well before using.

APPLE AND GREEN PEPPER PORK CHOPS

– Serves 2

4 boneless pork loin chops
salt and pepper, to taste
1 tablespoon vegetable oil
1/2 onion, sliced
1 leek, washed and sliced
1 tablespoon butter
1/2 green pepper, sliced
1 1/2 Granny Smith apples, peeled, cored and sliced
1/2 tablespoon paprika

1. Season the pork chops with salt and pepper.
2. Heat the oil in a heavy skillet on medium-high heat and brown pork chops on both sides. Remove from pan and set aside.
3. Add onion to the skillet and brown.
4. Return pork chops to pan and simmer for 15 minutes on each side.
5. In a medium sauce pan melt butter. Saute' leeks until lightly browned.
6. Add green pepper and apples. Sprinkle with paprika, salt and pepper and stir well.
7. Cover and simmer on low heat for 20 minutes.

SIMPLE POTATO CASSEROLE
– Serves 2

> 2 large baking potatoes
> 4 tablespoons butter, melted
> 4 tablespoons vegetable oil
> 1 clove garlic, minced
> 1/4 to 1/2 teaspoon salt
> 1/4 teaspoon dried thyme leaves

1. Cut potatoes into 1/4" thick slices.
2. Layer potato slices in buttered 9" x 13" baking dish.
3. Mix butter and oil. Brush potato slices with mixture. Pour remaining butter and oil mixture over potatoes and sprinkle with garlic, salt, and thyme.
4. Bake at 400° for 25 minutes or until potato edges are brown. Serve immediately.

STRAWBERRY PIE

– *Makes 1 pie*

"It tastes great. I love strawberries and yogurt."

> 1 baked pie shell, cooled
> 2 cups sweetened strawberries
> 1 cup plain yogurt
> 1 teaspoon honey
> 1/2 teaspoon vanilla
> 1 8-ounce package cream cheese

1. Pour sweetened strawberries into pie shell.
2. Whip yogurt, vanilla, honey, and cream cheese until consistency of whipped cream.
3. Pour mixture on top of strawberries and chill.

FRANK

} • Forty Something
• Retired
• Phoenix, Oregon

Hobbies and Interest . . .

"Learning to play the guitar for the third
time since 1965, and playing the keyboard.
Restoring classic American muscle cars
has been both a hobby and a passion for
fifteen years. I like camping, fishing,
canoeing on quiet mountain lakes, golfing,
racing my RC truck, building models, and
shooting pool."

Goals . . .

"To find someone to share it with. I hope to play the guitar and/or
keyboard and sing on stage someday. I want to perform a part on stage,
too. In a few years, when I build my own workshop, I plan to build an
airplane and at least one hot rod worthy of some car magazine."

– continued next page

Accomplishments . . .

"I am proud of the close relationship between myself and my 12 year old daughter and managing a 'rag tag' Little League baseball team. Restoring a 1973 Dodge Challenger that took a first place title and taking a second place title in a Corvette solo autocross last summer."

Philosophy of Life . . .

"99% of the people in this world have a good heart, but the 1% left over get all the media coverage. Friends can be made easily anywhere. Honesty and trust are the most important attributes a person can possess."

Ideal Woman . . .

"My ideal woman would have intelligence, honesty, trust, and humor. She would like all kinds of music, 'go fast' cars, long drives in the country, and quiet evenings at home. I prefer that she is between 5' and 5' 8" tall and no more than 150 pounds. Her hair, eye color, and race are unimportant."

Chicken Hawaiian
My Salad Confusion

CHICKEN HAWAIIAN

– Serves 2

"My mother gave this recipe to me several years ago. It is an excellent recipe for preparing chicken. I cook chicken many different ways and like them all. I couldn't pick just one as my favorite."

1/2 green pepper, cut in strips
1/2 garlic clove, minced
1 tablespoon salad oil
1/2 of a 13-ounce can pineapple tidbits, reserve 1/2 of juice

1 10 1/2-ounce can of cream of chicken soup
1/2 pound cooked chicken, cubed
1 tablespoon soy sauce
2 cups cooked rice
2 tablespoons toasted slivered almonds

1. In a 10" skillet, saute green pepper and garlic in oil over medium heat until tender.
2. Blend in reserved pineapple juice and soup.
3. Add chicken, pineapple tidbits, and soy sauce.
4. Heat to boiling, stirring occasionally.
5. Serve over rice and top with almonds.

147

MY SALAD CONFUSION
– Serves 2

> 2 cups fresh shredded lettuce
>
> 1 cup sliced carrots
>
> 1 cup chopped celery
>
> 1/4 cup diced green onion
>
> 1/2 cup sliced green or red pepper
>
> 1/2 cup sliced radishes
>
> 1/4 cup sliced cucumber

1. In a salad bowl, toss all ingredients, except cucumbers which are layered on top.
2. Serve with equal amounts of olive oil and wine vinegar or your favorite salad dressing.

FRITZ

- Thirty Something
- Machinist
- Medford, Oregon

Hobbies and Interests . . .

"Motorcycles and bicycles are my main hobbies. I also enjoy a little snow skiing. I'm a member of the YMCA and use the gym three days a week. I enjoy movies at the theater and I listen to rock, R&B, and some classical music. I also enjoy travel and sports events."

Goals . . .

"To enjoy life and hopefully make the lives of my friends and family richer."

Accomplishments . . .

"Becoming a home owner!"

– continued next page

Philosophy of Life . . .

"To enjoy and savor every moment of life and to take nothing and no one for granted."

Ideal Woman . . .

"Has honesty and integrity with a sense of humor."

Broccoli-Tato
Fritz's Quick and Easy Salad

BROCCOLI-TATO

– Serves 2

"This is a quick and simple nutritious dinner for someone who is short on time."

2 baking potatoes
1/2 cup fresh chopped broccoli
2 teaspoons butter
ranch style dressing, as desired

1. Clean and microwave potatoes 10 1/2 minutes, making sure to ventilate them by using a fork. Or, bake them in your oven at 350° for 45 minutes.
2. When done, open filet style on a plate and top each with 1 teaspoon butter and broccoli.
3. Serve with ranch dressing.

FRITZ'S QUICK AND EASY SALAD —————————————————

– *Serves 2*

1 8-ounce bag of pre-made salad
1/2 cup of fresh broccoli, cut into small pieces
1 6-ounce can tuna
 ranch or thousand island dressing, as desired

1. Mix all ingredients together.
2. Top with salad dressing. Serve with dinner rolls.

Variation: Substitute pre-made salad for an Instant Pasta Salad.

MARTIN

- Twenty Something
- Sales
- Milwaukie, Oregon

Hobbies and Interests . . .

"My hobbies and interests include a wide range of outdoor activities. I like running, but it doesn't like me. Golfing is where it's at, but I love water whether it be fresh or salt. I enjoy swimming, boarding, fishing, crabbing or just watching the sun set over the beach. Even though I like the water, the mountains are where I'm most relaxed. Fresh air and the view while hiking or camping... you just can't beat it."

Goals . . .

"To start my own company and enjoy life (Pretty easy, huh? Yea...right.)."

– *continued next page*

Accomplishments . . .

"The accomplishment I'm proudest of is serving four years in the United States Marine Corps. That's it for right now, but I have a huge 'to do list'."

Philosophy of Life . . .

"If it sucks, it's probably worth it. I work a lot, but I work for my future, and fingers crossed, it will come true. As James Taylor once sang, 'The secret to life is enjoying the passing of time...' I try, but it's hard."

Ideal Woman . . .

"The qualities my ideal women share are the ability to think beyond the restraints of their own opinions. They care for themselves as if they're extinct. Their tongue is witty and senses are sharp. They have enough charisma to be elegant even when embarrassed, and enough control to smile when angry. They must respect others and strive for the best in life, yet be content with simple commodities. They have knowledge to understand the difference between men and women, and the experience to recognize changing it is impossible...compromise is the only approach."

Martin's Dinner Menu

Chicken Cordon "Blues"
Mushrooms in Sherry with Cream Sauce
"Genie" Asparagus
Martin's Garlic French Bread

CHICKEN CORDON "BLUES"

– Serves 2

"I dreamed up the 'Blues' from a variety of cooking shows I watch on occasion. So, you can do the same. Put a layer of spinach in between each stack, change the ingredients, or do whatever 'floats your boat'. Have fun...that is the most important thing!"

> 1 whole extra large chicken breast, halves attached in middle
> 2 slices honey baked ham
>   (the deli slicer is set on #7 for lunch meat, use #12 for this recipe)
> 2 slices Swiss cheese
> 2 slices Havarti cheese

1. Remove fat from chicken.
2. Lay chicken breast flat and slice each section in half to form a pocket for stuffing, leaving pieces joined in the middle.
3. Stuff each chicken pocket with a slice of Havarti cheese and ham. Put Swiss cheese on top.
4. Bake at 425° for 35 to 45 minutes or bake on a barbecue grill over an aluminum lined deep dish pan to catch excess fat.
5. Remove from oven and slice and serve.

MUSHROOMS IN SHERRY WITH CREAM SAUCE

– Serves 2

1 large Portabela mushroom

3/4 cup cream sherry (I use Hartley & Gibson's)

1/2 cup heavy whipping cream

1 pinch dry mustard

1/2 teaspoon garlic powder

3 dashes white pepper

1. Slice mushroom into 1/4" slices. Place in a sauce pan and pour sherry over them. Cover and let marinate. Prepare the rest of the meal while mushrooms are marinating.

2. Cook mushrooms on high. As sherry starts to boil, tip pan to a 25° angle. Touch lip of pan with a match until it flames. As flame dies out, pour in cream and rest of dry ingredients.

3. Turn heat down to medium-high and cook for about 10 to 15 minutes, or until thick.

4. Place mushrooms and sauce over Chicken Cordon "Blues."

"GENIE" ASPARAGUS
– Serves 2

1 small stalk asparagus (8-10)
1 pinch dry mustard
10 dashes "Bon Appetit"
1/2 teaspoon garlic powder
3 pinches thyme
2 pinches dry ginger
1/4 cup low salt soy sauce
3 pinches each coriander, fennel, sage

1. Wash and trim asparagus and lay in sauce pan.
2. Combine dry ingredients and soy sauce, add to sauce pan.
3. Pour water into pan halfway up asparagus. Cook on high until liquid cooks dry.
4. When liquid is gone, shake pan over heat for two minutes. Serve immediately.

MARTIN'S GARLIC FRENCH BREAD
– Serves 2

1 small loaf French bread
olive oil
garlic powder, to taste

1. Heat oven to 400°.
2. Brush top of bread with oil. Sprinkle with garlic.
3. Wrap bread in foil for approximately 10 minutes.
4. Slice and serve.

"Cooking is a great way for me to relieve stress and be creative!"

JAMES

- Forty Something
- Carpenter/Plumber/Electrician
- Rogue River, Oregon

Hobbies and Interests . . .

"I like bicycle and motorcycle riding. I have three cats. I enjoy gardening, cooking, movies, and working with my tools and equipment. I collect German Opel cars, of which I have five. I enjoy picking wild blackberries and making my own blackberry preserves."

Goals . . .

" To design and build my own home. I'm working on the plans now and have cleared a building site on my property. I hope to start construction this year."

– *continued next page*

Accomplishments . . .

"The accomplishments I'm proudest of are my skills and expertise in all areas of construction. I also do all my own vehicle repair and maintenance. I pride myself on being able to design, build or repair almost anything."

Philosophy of Life . . .

"My philosophy is enjoy life. Try to pet every cat you happen to meet."

Ideal Woman . . .

"She must enjoy cats, be willing to work to accomplish her goals, be athletic, ambitious, and full of energy is a plus."

James' Dinner Menu

Spray Painted Chicken
Betty's Big Beautifully Bodacious Butter Biscuits
Candace's Fruit Salad
Jim's Special Cheesecake

SPRAY PAINTED CHICKEN

– Serves 4

"My own invention. Quick and easy to prepare. Don't knock it until you've tried it!"

1 fryer chicken
2 tablespoons vegetable oil
non-stick cooking spray
Lawry's seasoning salt, to taste
dash of pepper

1. Heat oven to 375°.
2. Put vegetable oil in a dutch oven or a large, heavy pot.
3. Wash the chicken and pat it dry.
4. Place chicken, breast side up, in pot. Spray with non-stick cooking spray. Do this in a well ventilated area.
5. Sprinkle the chicken with Lawry's seasoning salt and pepper. Put the lid on and bake for 2 hours.
6. Remove lid and brown for about 15 minutes. Serve with baked potatoes.

161

BETTY'S BIG BEAUTIFULLY BODACIOUS BUTTER BISCUITS

"I can take credit only for the name. This recipe was taught to me by the wife of a good friend of mine. They are very generous people, and Betty was kind enough to take the time to show me how to make them when I told her how much I enjoyed them. I serve them with wild blackberry jam that I make myself."

2 cups all-purpose flour
1/2 cup sugar
3 tablespoons baking powder
1/2 teaspoon salt

whole milk, quantity varies
2 tablespoons cooking oil
2 tablespoons butter or margarine

1. Heat oven to 425°.
2. In a large skillet, at least 12", place the oil and butter. Put skillet in the oven and melt the butter.
3. Mix dry ingredients together in a bowl. Add just enough milk to allow mixture to form a loose ball, it may be a little crumbly. Turn out onto floured surface, roll to a thickness of 1/2". Mixture may be sticky so use flour to coat surface of rolling pin, hands and counter.
4. Cut the dough into round pieces with a cookie cutter or knife.
5. Remove the skillet from the oven and place biscuits into the melted butter and oil turning once to coat both sides. Return the skillet to the oven.
6. Bake approximately 15 minutes or until golden brown.

CANDACE'S FRUIT SALAD ————————

– Serves 2

3 apples, peeled, cored and cubed
1 cup raisins
1 cup chopped walnuts
1/4 head red cabbage, chopped
1/4 head green cabbage, chopped
2 carrots, peeled and shredded
4 ounces coleslaw salad dressing

1. Combine all ingredients.
2. Refrigerate 30 minutes before serving.

JIM'S SPECIAL CHEESECAKE ————————————

– Makes 1 cheesecake

"This cheesecake rises when it cooks, so use a spring form cake pan to bake it."

For the crust:
1 1/2 cups graham cracker crumbs
1/4 pound butter

For the filling:
2 8-ounce packages cream cheese,
    room temperature
1 quart sour cream
4 eggs
1 1/2 cups sugar
1/2 teaspoon salt
1 teaspoon lemon extract
1 1/4 teaspoon vanilla

1. Mix butter and graham cracker crumbs and press into the bottom of a spring form pan.

2. Blend all ingredients together, mixture will be lumpy.

3. Pour filling on top of crust and bake at 350° for 1 1/4 hours.

4. Refrigerate for 24 hours before serving.

MATTHEW

- Thirty Something
- Consultant
- Medford, Oregon

Hobbies and Interests . . .

"My hobbies and interests include piano playing, long walks, hiking, swimming, and tennis. I enjoy picnics, also in the fall and winter, fires, and hot spas."

Goals . . .

"To meet each challenge as it comes, strive to continuously improve all aspects of life, and always respect my family members and their feelings."

Acoomplishments . . .

"Retiring from the United States Navy as a lieutenant, and receiving my MBA in International Business with highest honors!"

– continued next page

Philosophy of Life . . .

"Living day to day and enjoying every day to the fullest. Other people's happiness increases my happiness."

Ideal Woman . . .

"My ideal woman is intelligent, affectionate, attractive, fit, monogamous, open-minded, fun-loving, and sensitive."

Matthew's Dinner Menu

Herb & Parsley Salad
Pork Chops in White Wine & Mushroom Sauce
Rhubarb and Apple Pie

HERB AND PARSLEY SALAD

– Serves 2

"An exciting, flavorful starter bursting with fresh herbs and a light extra-virgin olive oil dressing. I enjoy this wonderful salad because of the bountiful taste that comes with every mouthful. I chose this salad due to the plethora of vitamins and minerals that accompany it's fresh, exciting taste."

1 1/2 cups tender, 1" curly leaf
   parsley sprigs
2/3 cup tender, 1" Italian parsley sprigs
1 cup chopped fresh basil leaves
2/3 cup 1" watercress sprigs
2 tablespoons minced fresh tarragon
2 tablespoons minced fresh marjoram leaves
1 tablespoon minced fresh sage leaves

3 tablespoons freshly grated
   Parmesan cheese
1 small clove garlic, minced
2 tablespoons extra-virgin olive oil
1 1/2 tablespoons water
1 tablespoon lemon juice
salt and pepper, to taste

1. Mix herbs, watercress, and Parmesan cheese.
2. In a tightly sealed container shake garlic, olive oil, water, and lemon juice until blended. Season with salt and pepper.
3. Add dressing to salad and gently toss. If making ahead of time, chill salad and dressing separately for up to 4 hours.
4. Serve with a nice Pinot Gris, Pinot Blanc, or Fume Blanc wine.

167

PORK CHOPS IN WHITE WINE AND MUSHROOM SAUCE

—*Serves 2*

"A thrilling, robust, high-protein main course. Served with steamed cauliflower and steamed rice, this course fulfills anyone's dietary and savory taste requirements. I enjoy this dish because it is easy to prepare and delightful to share. This dish was chosen for its ease of preparation, abundance of healthful nutrients, and wonderful flavor."

1 large onion, chopped	1/2 teaspoon celery salt
5 cloves garlic, minced	1/2 teaspoon black pepper
olive oil	1 egg (oil or milk may be substituted)
2 cans cream of mushroom soup	1 cup bread crumbs
2/3 cup white wine	2 lean pork chops

1. Saute' onion and garlic in a skillet with a small amount of olive oil.
2. Add cream of mushroom soup, wine, celery salt, and pepper. Stir and simmer for 10 minutes.
3. Remove from heat and pour into a baking dish big enough for two pork chops.
4. Trim fat from the pork chops.
5. Bread the chops on both sides by dipping them in egg and then in bread crumbs.
6. In a skillet, brown chops on both sides in olive oil. Place browned chops in baking dish on top of mushroom sauce. Spoon sauce onto chops to cover them.
7. Bake at 350° for 25 to 30 minutes.

RHUBARB AND APPLE PIE

—*Makes 1 pie*

"A scintillating combination of tart rhubarb and delicious apples merged to perfection. I enjoy this most titillating dessert because of its unique blend of tartness and sweetness in each delectable mouthful. This dessert was chosen for its complement to the main course, and its boldness provided at the end of the meal."

For the short crust pastry:

2 1/2 cups sifted all-purpose flour

1/2 teaspoon salt

6 tablespoons butter, cut into small pieces

6 tablespoons margarine

6 tablespoons cold water

For the filling:

2 cups rhubarb.
    cut diagonally into small pieces

2 cups apple cut into small pieces

1 1/2 cups sugar

2 tablespoons butter, cut into small pieces

grated rind of 1 orange

2 tablespoons cornstarch

1/4 cup orange juice

1/2 teaspoon cinnamon

2 tablespoons milk

– *continued next page* . . .

1. Sift the flour into a bowl. Add the salt and butter. Cut the butter into the flour until it is pea size. Blend in the margarine.

2. Stir in the cold water with a fork adding 4 tablespoons first and then 1 tablespoon at a time. Add only enough water to form the dough into a ball. Wrap ball in wax paper and chill 20 minutes.

3. Cut the pastry in half and roll out on lightly floured board. Fit into a 9" pie plate.

4. Put rhubarb, apples, sugar, butter, and orange rind into pastry shell. Dissolve cornstarch and cinnamon in orange juice, then pour into pastry shell.

5. Cover with a second round of pastry. Brush top crust with milk.

6. Bake at 375° for 30 minutes or until crust is golden. Serve warm or cold with sweetened whipped cream.

NORMAN

- Fifty Something
- Equipment Operator/Mechanic
- Gold Hill, Oregon

Hobbies and Interests . . .

"I like to design and make things. I enjoy being outdoors, photography, helping friends, quiet times at home, and learning new things. I am presently completing a coffee table and matching end tables of black walnut that I started from a log."

Goals . . .

"My main goal is to find a lady that by working together, we can have many years of happiness. We can go places and do things together."

Accomplishments . . .

"I served my country for over 5 years in the United States Air Force in the United States and Germany."

– continued next page

Philosophy of Life . . .

"You help others and treat them with fairness and honesty and they will do the same for you."

Ideal Woman . . .

"My ideal lady is over 5'6", average build, as I have found that I am not attracted to heavy set ladies, a non-smoker, and one who enjoys her home...doesn't have to be out all of the time. I want a person who enjoys being in the country and likes to see new things and places. She should be 48-55 years old."

Pork Chop Casserole
A Special Treat

PORK CHOP CASSEROLE

– Serves 2-4

5 medium potatoes, sliced (fills 1/2 of casserole dish)

2 cans cream of mushroom soup

1 2" slice of cheddar cheese, shredded

1 large onion, chopped

1 teaspoon garlic powder

4 hot peppers, finely chopped

4 pork chops

1. Cover the bottom of a 9" x 9" casserole dish with a non-stick cooking spray then layer the potatoes.
2. Mix remaining ingredients in a bowl, excluding pork chops. (Do not dilute soup.)
3. Spread mix over potatoes and top with the pork chops.
4. Bake at 350° for 1 1/2 hours or until tender.

Variation: In the past I have used short ribs,
round steak and boneless country style spare ribs in place of pork chops.
Short ribs and spare ribs are placed in a pressure cooker for 5 minutes to tenderize.

A SPECIAL TREAT

"My mother who has been gone for 30 years used to make this at Christmas. It is very rich and a little goes a long way."

2 cans of Borden Eagle Brand sweetened condensed milk or
    Carnation sweetened condensed milk
1/2 cup miniature marshmallows
1/2 cup chopped dates
1/4 cup chopped nuts

1. Place cans of milk in a kettle, cover with water and boil three hours. Cool.
2. Open cans and transfer milk from container into two bowls.
3. Mix marshmallows, dates, and nuts between both dishes. Enjoy!

GREG

- Thirty Something
- Self Employed
- Portland, Oregon

Hobbies and Interests . . .

"Cooking, of course, candles, mountain biking, roller blading, camping, visiting Portland's Saturday Market, riding my Harley, attending gallery showings, going to the beach, romantic dinners and more romantic dinners."

Goals . . .

"To stay happy, find my soul mate, travel, and vacation with the one I love."

Accomplishments . . .

"My daughter who is 12 1/2 years old, an honor roll student, and has been in ballet for the last 7 years."

– continued next page

Philosophy of Life . . .

"My philosophy of life is it's short so enjoy it!"

Ideal Woman . . .

"To be happy with herself, funny, attractive, eclectic, creative, and romantic. My ideal woman would be my best friend forever. Did I mention she would be romantic?"

Greg's Dinner Menu

Green Salad with Dressing
B.B.Q Grilled Ahi with Pineapple Salsa
Greg's Twice Baked Potatoes

GREEN SALAD WITH DRESSING ——————————————

– Serves 2

green lettuce, enough for 2 salads
red lettuce, enough for 2 salads
1 chive, finely chopped
1/2 red bell pepper, diced

SALAD DRESSING

1/4 cup extra virgin olive oil
1/4 cup gourmet seasoned rice wine vinegar
1 tablespoon chopped fresh lemon thyme

1. Toss lettuce and vegetables together.
2. Mix ingredients for dressing and pour over salad. Serve on a chilled plate.

B.B.Q GRILLED AHI WITH PINEAPPLE SALSA

– Serves 2

2 ahi fish fillets

Hawaiian style soy sauce, as desired

1/2 cup finely diced pineapple

1/4 cup chopped white onion

1/4 cup chopped red bell pepper

2 tablespoons finely chopped cilantro

1 jalapeno pepper, minced

1 tablespoon sugar

1. Season ahi with soy sauce.
2. Sear ahi over hot coals on barbebcue grill until medium done, approximately 6 minutes per inch of thickness.
3. Mix ingredients of salsa in any order and chill.
4. When fish is ready, serve with salsa.

GREG'S TWICE BAKED POTATOES
– *Serves 2*

2 large baking potatoes

2 teaspoons butter

onion powder, as desired

1/3 cup grated cheddar cheese

1/3 cup Imo-Chivo (baked potato topping)

2 teaspoons sherry

1/2 teaspoon minced fresh garlic

1/4 teaspoon salt

paprika, to taste

1. Scrub potatoes and dry. Pierce several times with a fork.
2. Rub each potato with 1 teaspoon of butter and dust lightly with onion powder.
3. Bake at 425° for 45 minutes.
4. Remove potatoes and cut off top 1/3 from each potato. Cool.
5. Scoop out potato pulp with metal spoon and place in a large mixing bowl, add remaining ingredients and mash together well.
6. Spoon mixture back into potato shells and top with a dash of paprika.
7. Return to oven and bake at 425° for another 20 to 25 minutes or until lightly browned.

—INDEX—

ahi, barbecued grilled with pineapple salsa, 178
apple:
    apple and green pepper pork chops, 142
    apple pie bars, 56
    apple raisin quiche, 129
    carrot apple delight soup, 49
    rhubarb and apple pie, 169
    turkey and apple sausage, 38
apple and green pepper pork chops, 142
apple pie bars, 56
apple raisin quiche, 129
asparagus, "Genie", 157
beef:
    burritos, quick-n-easy breakfast, 19
    pizza, Mark's, 55
beverages:
    blender mix, Bob's, 27
    lemon lush, 73
    milky way coffee, 61
    smoothie, Ben and Bailey's, 52
    tomato sipper, spicy, 40
blender mix, Bob's, 27
bread:
    butter biscuits, Betty's big
        beautiful bodacious, 162
    cheese bread, 66
    focaccia, 111
    French toast, 21
    garlic bread, David's, 124
    garlic bread, Mark's, 82
    garlic French bread, Martin's, 158
    pineapple pumpkin bread, 50
    zucchini bread, moist, 87
broccoli-tato, 151
burritos, quick-n-easy breakfast, 19

carrot apple delight soup, 49
cheese:
    blue cheese salad with mustard chive
        dressing, 141
    cheesecake, Jim's special, 164
    cheese bread, 66
    cottage cheese pancakes, 11
    hazelnut cheesecake with huckleberry
        sauce, 112
    Parmesan zucchini, 106
    peanut mousse cheese pie, 51
    quiche, Roger's fantastic, 72
cheese bread, 66
cheesecake, Jim's special, 164
chicken:
    chicken cordon "blues" with sherry
        cream sauce, 155
    chicken Hawaiian, 147
    chicken stoup, 65
    chicken, spray painted, 161
    chicken Yoshida's, 46
    honey and orange chicken, 117
chicken cordon "blues" with sherry cream
    sauce, 155
chicken Hawaiian, 147
chicken stoup, 65
chicken, spray painted, 161
chicken Yoshida's, 46
chocolate massacre, Texas, 137
consomme' with carrots, Japanese, 91
corn on the cob, grilled, 123
cornmeal griddle cakes with
    strawberry sauce, southern, 31
coshe, 86
cottage cheese pancakes, 11

desserts:
    apple pie bars, 56
    cheesecake, Jim's special, 164
    chocolate massacre, Texas, 137
    hazelnut cheesecake with
        huckleberry sauce, 112
    peach shortcake, 37
    peanut mousse cheese pie, 51
    rhubarb and apple pie, 169
    rice pudding, 67
    special treat, 174
    strawberry pie, 144
duck salad, warm, 135
Dungeness crab pancakes, 133
eggplant Parmesan, 81
eggs:
    apple raisin quiche, 129
    eggs, good, 33
    mountain machako, 77
    omelette, deluxe, 25
    omelette, Jeff's lowfat weekend booster, 7
    quiche, Roger's fantastic, 72
    salmon omelette, smoked, 15
eggs, good, 33
fish:
    ahi, barbecued grilled with
        pineapple salsa, 178
    salmon, barbecued, 121
    salmon, barbecued teriyaki, 105
    salmon, omelette, smoked, 15
flapjacks, 20
focaccia, 111
French fries, "almost" fat free, 8

French toast, 21
fruit:
    apple and green pepper pork chops, 142
    apple pie bars, 56
    apple raisin quiche, 129
    blender mix, Bob's, 27
    carrot apple delight soup, 49
    fruit bowl, tropical, 16
    fruit salad, 12
    fruit salad, Candace's, 163
    honey and orange chicken, 117
    melon wraps, 99
    peach shortcake, 37
    pineapple pumpkin bread, 50
    rhubarb and apple pie, 169
    strawberry pie, 144
    strawberry sauce, 32
    turkey and apple sausage, 38
fruit bowl, tropical, 16
fruit salad, 12
fruit salad, Candace's, 163
garlic bread, David's, 124
garlic bread, Mark's, 82
garlic French bread, Martin's, 158
gazpacho soup, cold, 98
Grape Nuts, hot, 39
green beans, sauteed, 122
green salad with dressing, 177
hazelnut cheesecake with huckleberry sauce, 112
honey and orange chicken, 117
honey mustard vegetables, 118
huckleberry sauce, 113
lamb, roast rack with mint pesto crust, 136
lemon lush, 73

lentil soup with ham hocks, 78
machako, mountain, 77
melon wraps, 99
milky way coffee, 61
mushrooms and wine sauce, 128
mushrooms in sherry with cream sauce, 156
mushrooms, fried, 59
mushrooms, stuffed, 93
omelette, deluxe, 25
omelette, Jeff's lowfat weekend booster, 7
pancakes:
    cornmeal griddle cakes, southern
        with strawberry sauce, 31
    cottage cheese pancakes, 11
    Dungeness crab pancakes, 133
    flapjacks, 20
parsley and herb salad, 167
pasta:
    scallop and prawns flavious, 110
    spaghetti carbonara, 127
peach shortcake, 37
peanut mousse cheese pie, 51
pheasant, Amontillado, 85
pineapple pumpkin bread, 50
pizza, Mark's, 55
pork:
    apple and green pepper pork chops, 142
    pork chop casserole, 173
    pork chops in white wine and
        mushroom sauce, 168
pork chop casserole, 173
pork chops in white wine and
   mushroom sauce, 168
porridge, papa's, 26

potato casserole, simple, 143
potatoes, Greg's twice baked, 179
potatoes:
    broccoli-tato, 151
    coshe, 86
    French fries, "almost" fat free, 8
    potato casserole, simple, 143
    potatoes, Greg's twice baked, 179
poultry:
    pheasant, Amontillado, 85
    chicken cordon "blues" with
        sherry cream sauce, 155
    chicken Hawaiian, 147
    chicken stoup, 65
    chicken, spray painted, 161
    chicken Yoshida's, 46
    duck salad, warm, 135
    honey and orange chicken, 117
    turkey and apple sausage, 38
prawns, Tex-Mex, 97
quiche:
    apple raisin quiche, 129
    quiche, Roger's fantastic, 72
rhubarb and apple pie, 169
rice pudding, 67
roast rack of lamb with mint pesto crust, 136
saffron sauce, 134
salad, confusion, 148
salad, Fritz's quick and easy, 152
salads:
    blue cheese salad with
        mustard chive dressing,141
    duck salad, warm, 135
    fruit bowl, tropical, 16

fruit salad, 12
fruit salad, Candace's, 163
green salad with dressing, 177
my salad confusion, 148
parsley and herb salad, 167
salad, Frtiz's quick-n-easy, 152
spinach salad, 71
spinach salad with hot bacon dressing, 109
tofu salad, 92
salmon, barbecued, 121
salmon, barbecued teriyaki, 105
salmon omelette, smoked, 15
salsa:
    pineapple salsa, 178
sauces:
    huckelberry sauce, 113
    saffron sauce, 134
    strawberry sauce, 32
scallop and prawns flavious, 110
seafood:
    ahi, barbecued grilled with
        pineapple salsa, 178
    Dungeness crab pancakes, 133
    prawns, Tex-Mex, 97
    salmon, barbecued, 121
    salmon, barbecued teriyaki, 105
    salmon omelette, smoked, 15
    scallop and prawns flavious, 110
smoothie, Ben and Bailey's, 52
soups / stews:
    carrot apple delight soup, 49
    chicken stoup, 65
    consomme' with carrots, Japanese, 91
    gazpacho soup, cold, 98

    lentil soup with ham hocks, 78
    tomato and rice soup, 60
spaghetti carbonara, 127
special treat, 174
spinach salad, 71
spinach salad with hot bacon dressing, 109
squash, spectacular, 45
strawberry pie, 144
strawberry sauce, 32
tofu salad, 92
tomato and rice soup, 60
tomato sipper, spicy, 40
turkey and apple sausage, 38
vegetables:
    asparagus, "Genie", 157
    corn of the cob, grilled, 123
    coshe, 86
    eggplant, Parmesan, 81
    French fries, "almost" fat free, 8
    green beans, sauteed, 122
    honey mustard vegetables, 118
    mushrooms and wine sauce, 128
    mushrooms, fried, 59
    mushrooms in sherry with cream sauce, 156
    mushrooms, stuffed, 93
    pork chop casserole, 173
    potato casserole, simple, 143
    potatoes, Greg's twice baked, 179
    squash, spectacular, 45
    zucchini bread, moist, 87
    zucchini, Parmesan, 106
venison:
    mountain machako, 77
zucchini, Parmesan, 106
zucchini bread, moist, 87

BOOK ORDERING INFORMATION

MAIL TO: **Good Cookin' Bachelors**

1133 South Riverside, Suite 10-122

Medford, OR 97501-7807

PHONE ORDERS: (541) 773-7160 **INTERNET ORDERS:** http://www.goodcookinbachelors.com

Please send _____ copies of *Good Cookin' Bachelors Cookbook* to the following:

NAME _____

ADDRESS _____

CITY _____ STATE _____ ZIP _____

PHONE (   ) _____

BOOK:

$16.95 each, U.S. Funds

POSTAGE AND HANDLING:

$3.00 for the first book and .75 cents for each additional book, delivered to the same address.

PAYMENT: (Please check one)

☐ Check   ☐ Money Order   ☐ Cashiers Check   ☐ VISA   ☐ MasterCard

Credit Card No. | | | | | | | | | | | | | | | | |

Authorized signature _____ Expiration date: ____/_____

GIFT DELIVERY:

NAME _____

ADDRESS _____

CITY _____ STATE _____ ZIP _____

PHONE (   ) _____

For quantity discounts, please contact the author(s)
at the above address or call (541) 773-7160

Thank You

5% of all profits from the sale of *Good Cookin' Bachelors Cookbook* will go to the Oregon Coalition Against Domestic and Sexual Violence